SURIVAL: THE ULTIM

CU00641597

"The problems which confront us to
They have no counterparts in hum
pages of history for solutions, for p

This, then, is the ultimate challeng
survival, for the answers, to the questions
which have never before been posed?

We must look, first to Almighty God, who has raised
man above the animals and endowed him with intelligence
and reason; we must put our faith in him, that he will not
desert us or permit us to destroy humanity which he
created in his image.

We must look into ourselves, into the depth of our souls.
We must become something we have never been
and for which our education and experience and
environment have ill-prepared us.

We must become bigger than we have been.
More courageous, greater in spirit, larger in outlook.
We must become members of a new race,
overcoming petty prejudice, owing our ultimate allegiance
not to nations but to our fellow men within the human community."

Oct, 6th 1963 - From H.I.M. Address to the United Nations

(p.377 Selected Speeches of H.I.M.)

These scripts feature the precepts of the House of Nyahbinghì Inl Iritual Ivictions.

The Rapture Nyahbinghì Reincarnation irits on earth to a place called Zion in Ethiopia Camp David Ancient Dominion Empire ene ena ene kafetannahg selt'anaccen naw

Preface

All praises to Germawi Negusa Nagast Qadamawi Haile Selassie 1st, Christ in his kingly character, King Ras Tafari of Ethiopia.

Inl book is livicated to all those whose sins have been forgiven, Ras Boanerges, Prince Nan and all Inl ingels, also the revolutionaries warriors that battled against the USA invasion of Grenada, the forces of president Ronald Reagan, he that William Peter Blanty, in his book 'The Exorcist' revealed to be the anti-Christ and most of all the revolutionaries warriors who tore down the principles of Mariam Mengist, Egzer Yemasgan.

Touch not mine anointed
And do my prophets no harm,

NYAHBINGHI known as
THE RAPTURE

Glory be to the word
Glory be to sound
Glory be to the power of the I AM that I AM
Supreme architect Christ in his kingly character
Haile Selassie 1st
Janhoy King Ras Tafari

This world is not InI home InI are only passing through, all our treasures are in heavenly Zion beyond the seven seals, q'esocc wayem nabiyocc karom yallam.

The spirit of the world dressing language, music and lifestyle all belonging to the colonial slave master and the Anglophone Caribbean.

ጸሎት ።

TSE-LOT
Prayer

እግታችን፡ሀዖይ ፣ በሰማዖ ፡ የምትኖር ፤

ABBA-TA-CHIN HOY
Oh Our FATHER

BESEM-MAY
In Heaven

YEMIT-NOR
Who Lives

ስም ህ ፡ ይቀደስ ፡ መንግሥትህ ፡ ትምጣ ።

SIM-MIH
Your Name

YIQ-QEDES
Is Holy

MEN-GISH-TIH
Your Rulership

TIM-TTA
Is To Come

ፈቃድህ ፡ በሰማዖ ፡ እንደሆነች ፤

FEQ-QAAD-DIH'
Your Will

BESEM-MAY
In Heaven

INDE-HONECH
Like, As She Became

እንደ ሁ ፡ በምድር ፡ ትሁን ።

IN-DEEHU
Like This

BEM-MIDIR
In Earth

TI-HUN
To Be

የዕለት ፡ እንጀራችንን ፡ ስጠን ፡ ዛሬ ።

YE'IL-LET
Of Day; Daily

IN-JERA-CHININ
Our Bread

SITTEN
Give Us

ZA-REY
To Day

በደላችንንም ፡ ይቅር ፣ በለን ፤ እኛ ፡

BEDELA-CHIN-NIM
Our Wrongdoings

YIQ-QIR
Excuse, Forgive

BEL-LEN
For Us

IÑ-ÑAA
We

የበደሉንን ፡ ይቅር ፡ እንደምንል ።

YEBEDEL-LUNIN
They Who Wrong Us

YIQ-QIR
Excuse

INDE-MINIL
Like, As We

ወደ ፈተናም ፡ አታግባን ፤

WEDE-FETEN-NAM
Towards Temptation

AT-TAAG-BAAN
We Will Not Enter

ከክፉ ፡ እድነን ፡ እንጂ ።

KE-KIF-FU
From The Evil

ADIN-NIN
We Are Saved

IN-JEE
On The Other Hand/ But

መንግሥት ፡ ያንተ ፡ ናትና ።

MEN-GISHT
the Rulership

YAN-TE
Yours

NAT-TIN-NA
For She Is

ኃይልም ፡ ምስጋናም ፡ ለዘለዓለሙ ።

HAY-YILIM
And Power

MIS-GAAN-NAAM
And Thanks/ Praise

LEZEL-E-'AAL'EM-MU
Are Forever/ World
Without End

አሜን ።

AM-MEYN.
The True And Faithful Witness

The Rapture is the second appearance of I Negus I Christ on earth in his kingly character King of Kings, Lord of Lords conquering lion of Judah, elect of God, earth's rightful ruler, decent of King David and Solomon, H. I. M emperor Haile Selassie 1st, Ras Tafari Makonnen of Ethiopia with his Ingels InI Nyahbinghi I: in a twinkle of an eye a trumpet shall sound proclaiming the return of the Christ in his kingly character. Then those that have eye (spiritual eye) i.e. the dead in Christ shall rise up and live with the returned Messiah.

His honour and glory shall be through all of the earth that every ear shall hear. On that bright and glorious morning when the raptured shall be gathered, we shall fly away home, whether in body or spirit, we shall be away from worldly desires.

The spirit of the world shall be dead and the spirit of Christ in his Kingly character the I AM THAT I AM shall live. The will of men shall be no more, the will of the almighty supreme architect shall rein Icracy Iternal.

Through lightening, through thunder, through landslides, brimstone, earthquake, whirlwinds and tidal waves the oppressors shall be no more.

Contents

Chapter One

The Rapture: Reincarnation Nyahbinghì

Nyahbinghì faith, *the rapture*, is a reincarnation of the dead spirit of the world, reincarnated unto life in Ivine livity spiritual soul transition - transmigration: *a deed of transporting a person's spirit (soul Irits) from one sphere of existence to another i.e. from an all earth material worldly spirit sense to a cosmic Ivine spiritual knowledge*, heavenly in Mount Zion' reincarnation is in great height: spiritual knowledge powers. The reincarnation of the dead spirit Irits of the world through Nyahbinghì, *the rapture*, fire baptism takes place at the Nyahbinghì Tabernacle.

In the soul Irits where it is revealed, handed down, recognised and sealed for what a man Iritcally carries in Iviction that he becomes. The spirit is reincarnated unto immortality *Ivinity* being released from the dead concepts of the world.

Reincarnation of the soul Irits in the living body the soul transmigrates through essence cosmic principle powers. Now InI raptured soul irits can only live in Mount Zion as InI pilgrimage to the Rastafari house, giving thanks and *isis* for the appearance of Christ in his kingly character Emperor Haile Selassie 1st Everyday becomes the king's hola Sabbath. In InI reincarnation all that is moved is ones heart and soul desires, those desires that were given to ones by the ways and concepts of the world.

There is no death in *the rapture* Nyahbinghì faith only material decay and change. The earthly body is not permanent whereas the living I lives forIver. The body is not considered as I in InI cosmic tradition for the ever living I is not earth material. When a one addresses another as I, it's not the object person the word sound is addressing but the Irits which has a cosmic appearance as the image of the body same as InI transcendental form of cosmology, therefore InI tradition is a cosmic tradition.

Wherever a person dwells on earth and holds the concept 'that the manifestation of the body was their beginning and when the body gets old or whenever it cease to function, that is their end,' such persons are of only worldly material sense. They are the living dead concepts of the world spirit, they might have sat in a church building all the days that their body functioned or went on an intellectual spree with the spirit of the world that is dead in Christ in his kingly character.

They had been spiritually dead 'the living dead' they serve the dragon, the beast, the anti-Christ and the whore of Babylon those that have signed the Sini covenant the camp David agreement in America.

The second appearance of Christ on earth is what's called *the rapture*, Christ in his kingly character has come with InI Nyahbinghì to rescue those who have refused Babylon evil world's captivity, the resistance against satanic teachings and annihilation, and waited on Imajesty Christ in his kingly character Emperor Haile Selassie 1st to bring judgment on the world through the Davidical sovereign throne of King Ras Tafari his dominion and powers.

All those who have put their personal life before the will of the maker of heaven and earth, those who instead of inquiring inward in the Nyahbinghi faith administration within themselves within the knowledge of knowing the Christ in his kingly character Ras Tafari: those who instead sorted the end tail of work feeding Babylon and receiving their less subsequently losing their soul in their attempt to buying the world's friendship.

These are the things that are not of the teachings of the world but are Inl faith, the world does not publish that Haile Selassie 1st is Christ in his kingly character. The world does not reveal that Ronald Reagan is the anti-Christ and that the movie world is the shrine of the anti-Christ.

The world does not teach that the Pope of Rome is the beast, the world does not expose that the head of Lucifer administration in the earth is the American administration. The world keeps it a secret mystery that the Queen of Buckingham is the great harlot of Babylon. Again I tell you that people of the world do not have Nyahbinghi faith, they carry not the Irits of Nyahbinghi they have not the Irits of *the rapture* faith.

When one's are bound to the things and life style of the ways of the world they are in bondage, Inl *the rapture* are cosmic appearance a separation from the world the concepts of the world birth, death, it enslaves your free will to the world, Inl cosmic order has no dualism one cannot serve the world whilst trodding Nyahbinghi.

Touch not mine anointed and do my prophets no harm, psalm 105:v15

Nyahbinghì faith for Recognition in the modern world

Inl Nyahbinghì are the Ingels – saints - who have come forward in this time from Mount Zion heavenly assembly, cosmic tradition together with Imajesty Christ in his kingly character Ras Tafari Makonnen, he manifested on earth in Ethiopia in 1892, Egzer Yemasgan.

Revelation chapter 4:v1-4, *'after this I looked, and behold, a door was opened in heaven and the first voice which I heard was as it were of a trumpet talking with me, which said, come up hither, and I will shew thee things which must be hereafter, and immediately I was in the spirit, and behold, a throne was set in heaven, and one sat on the throne, and he that sat was to look upon like a jasper and a sardine stone, and there was a rainbow round about the throne, in sight like unto an emerald, and round about the throne were four and twenty seats, and upon the seats I saw four and twenty elders sitting, clothed in white raiment, and they had on their heads crowns of gold…'*

Revelation chapter 5:v11, *'and I beheld, and I heard the voices of many ingels round about the throne and beast and elders, and the number of them was ten thousand times ten thousand, and thousands of thousands.'*

This portion Inl Nyahbinghì claim, is known as *the rapture* in Inl heavenly assembly Nyahbinghì faith is the fullness of Rastafari way of life on earth. One of the nominations of Rastafarian way of life, administering the ancient dominion Empire from Zion Ethiopian way of life, Inl cosmic tradition *the rapture*, Nyahbinghì not known to the world.

Jude chapter 1:v14, *'and Enoch also, the seventh from Adam, prophesied of these, saying behold the lord cometh with ten thousand of his saints, Christ in his kingly character, Haile Selassie 1st in his second advent,'* keeping his promise to the apostles. Also recorded by the prophets of the old testament, *'times when he shall make himself visible to the eyes of men, all inhabitants of the earth, that have eyes shall see him.'*

Inl Nyahbinghì known as *the rapture* the appearance of Christ in his kingly character, with Inl his hola Ingels – saints - to gather together those that have made a separation from the world all into one place. There where the Ark of the Covenant also the throne of David dwells, Ethiopia (the new Irusalam) Africa land, until the time of restoration into the world to come unto life Iternal.

The rapture – Nyahbinghì - is Inl faith that is Ivinely begotten through Imajesty Ras Tafari return in his kingly character and the gathering of Inl. Nyahbinghì is Inl faith our faith of *the rapture* of Christ in his kingly character, the black messiah imajesty Haile Selassie 1st, the head and only leader of those that are recorded in the high supreme authority in camp David ancient dominion Empire.

Giving thanks and Isis to the almighty of Shem Melchizedek, who blessed Abram, the same supreme architect of Isaac, Israel, David, Solomon and I Negus I Christ of

Bethlehem, is the same king Christ of Ethiopia, the 1st Haile Selassie in his kingly character.

Nyahbinghì Inl *the rapture* are the heavenly warriors, an army of fire *i*ngels reincarnated in icracy ivinity, king Ras Tafari Nyahbinghì Tabernacle administration, living in the ivine love prepared by Christ Imajesty Haile Selassie 1st, through Iditating_and searching Inl administration livity, within the third eye. Giving Isis from the eye and all the glory to Christ in his kingly character Haile Selassie the 1st and chanting death and judgment to white and black oppressors. Focusing Inl Iditation on self itrol through the third I and not turning the big wheel of the oppressors, justification of action and speech, whose message are ones really carrying now *word sound is always power.*

The world is dead in I Negus I Christ, the worldlians living on food for thought of the worldly ways, is a vampire not living on hola food for thought, but being inspired on the forges of the world, conception of men leadership and upmanship.

As Christ was the first born of the dead, (before now and forIver), first born living, knowing the heavenly father spiritually, Inl are the reincarnation of the dead in spirit of I Negus I Christ irits, now living following Imajesty Christ in his kingly character Ras Tafari.

Inl were manifested materially in earth, born to the world knowing only material senses, the body and object senses of the world. Inl reincarnation of that worldly spirit, that was dead to the obedience for the maker of heaven and earth. Ever since Adam and Eve ate the intellectual fruit and turned away from the Ivine diagnoses of the supreme architect, joining Christ Ras Tafari is the meaning of coming with Christ Imajesty Haile Selassie 1st.

Inl *the rapture* reincarnate Nyahbinghì from the dead in-spirit comes to an Ivine livity, given in the Nyahbinghì fire baptism of the rapture of Christ in his kingly character.

The seven seals loose from the bonds of the world: The six senses of material objects, the sense organs of the flesh. These six sense organs are all burning ears, eyes, nose, tongue, body and mind. The world is heaping up logs of desires coals burning of illusion and hatred.

The six objects of senses are on fire, form, sound, smell, touch, taste and objects of mind are all on fire. The six consciousness, sight, hearing, smell, taste, feelings and thoughts, are all in the melting pot.

Birth, death, pain, anxiety, frustration, worry, fear, despair every feelings of the world, whether pleasant or unpleasant shall be flushed in the tomb. They all arise because of concepts, concepts of the world not of truths, they are all conditioned by the senses organs, object of sense and sense consciousness, these are all worldly things, that are not Ivine immortal and are not the treasures of I rapture.

The spirit (Irits) of light is called the immortal, i.e.' *there is no night in Mount Zion; the rapture is the crown of glory of the Nyahbinghì. For Nyahbinghì was in earth but received the glory when the rapture came and declared being the Ingels of Iternal heaven through reincarnation within the rapture of Christ in his kingly character InI Iternal faith.'*

2nd Corinthians chapter 4v18,*'while we look not at the things which are seen, but the things which are not seen, for the things which are seen are temporal, but the things which are not seen are eternal.'*

In the time of Christ in his Kingly character and InI the hola ones only the Iternal in InI can lead InI to the Iternal, these are I essence cosmic principles that are Iternal, should one choose to live consumed in material sense, not knowing spiritual essence worth, the hola world to come one will not enter, at the time of *the rapture.*

Epistle of Jude1:v14,*'and Enoch also, the seventh from Adam, prophesied of these, say, behold, the lord cometh with ten thousand of his saints.'*

The fact that Imajesty king Christ comes on earth in his kingly character and InI recognize him that alone is not the complete fulfilment of all what's to happen in these times, for the reasons that most people of Rastafari way of life seem to want to celebrate in a worldly way, suggesting that's all there is to Rastafari way of life.

Acknowledging Christ in his kingly character but living as the world, 'No that's not!' for InI world in earth has to be built in and on lands that are not of or either in Gentile authorities.

Christ in his kingly character Ras Tafari, comes forward in judgment,' *for the coming of Christ in his kingly character in the rapture is judgment, see the precepts of the house of Nyahbinghì, prepared by Ikael Tafari hand in hand with Bongo Wattu and the knowledge Ingels in the Nyahbinghì administration.'*

Again Jude says more about *the rapture* - the epistle of Jude1:v15, *'to execute judgment upon all and to convince all that are ungodly among them of all their ungodly deeds, which they have ungodly committed and of all their hard speeches which ungodly sinners have spoken against him,'*

These are the days for InI to forget, let go the things and the ways of the world, these are the days that InI stop following other nations customs and tradition. Right now many ones cares for the world, their social obligations in Roman democracy, many stay back in the world, because of family ties with dead material sense relatives, *'reason for cause they say'.* Those that choose the world before king Ras Tafari; these are they that are running away from King Ras Tafari. Why is it that they are running away from King Ras Tafari, on their last judgement day, they must get paid? Their worldly occupation, their personal concept of material sense has nothing to do with *the rapture.*

Nyahbinghì isn't about man and women, it's about the administration, administering InI ancient Dominion Empire in Ivinity through word sound powers in cosmic principles, only those that are gathered beyond the fire of reincarnation, separation from Roman world, only through the fire baptism that one can reach there.

There are the thrones of the house of King David which InI the 24 elders and the 12 apostles sits, 'in a place called Zion, in Ethiopia, camp David ancient dominion empire. Iritcally today – everyday - when InI gather together and administer Nyahbinghì, the administration functions InI ancient dominion empire, in Ivinity.

InI supreme authority through the Nyahbinghì, the powers of the cosmic forces, unseen forces, that possess material for good and evil, not the individual that it possesses, but the force itself in the house of the rising sun. If Nyahbinghì was about man and women ones would go and call people, in the way of preaching it in the road, but it is not a central administration, going through the societies of the world, but InI administration judgments', does determine the course of the world.

Many ones that do not know Nyahbinghì administration think that the Nyahbinghì is about this one and that one and about themselves, no the Nyahbinghì is about the administration.

Love and cherish InI administration, ones must drive the administration for it is InI supreme authority, from the original way of the world iration, administering in Ivinity, walking in Ivinity in Zion, Ethiopia Camp David ancient dominion empire.

Administering unto the nations of Shem Ham and Japheth in judgement, InI seats of judgment are 'the thrones of the house of King David.' Ones need to search their heavens and find those cities, rebuild, populate and dwell therein; those ancient cities are InI heavens - mind structure - that InI carry.

It is not about organizations in the establish world because the cities in the Babylon world, NY, Paris, Tokyo, etc. are Roman Babylon, InI have cities, Solomanic cities of Judah and Israel, greater cities where there is no leaders except Haile Selassie the1st Christ in his kingly character.

InI that has been sanctified through the tabernacle, separated from the world through reincarnation, just us the administration that holds the authority of my way of life, InI are not dogmatic as those caught up in the world, but InI are caught up in *the rapture*, a state beyond the everyday social order.

On renouncement of the world, one has to have the fire baptism that only can happen in a Nyahbinghì tabernacle bestowed decorations and many of furnishings, from the free will heart of Nyahbinghì love Ingels in communication with king Christ Ras Tafari, Nyahbinghì administration in Sälam Irusalem within Mount Zion gates, that such one shall enter, be brought in by administering Ingels because ancient cities 'knowledge' has to be handed down, 'only at that time through the tabernacle that authority can be received, "real authority is Ivine". Those who did not enter Rastafari life through the tabernacle have no authority in this life.

Rastafari, organizations in the world authority is not authority; not Nyahbinghì administration Camp David Supreme authority of Mount Zion; there is my way of life InI are a million miles away from evil.

I word that not one or any skill or trade developed in the world before following king Christ Ras Tafari do not equip InI in this trod. It is a mystical cosmic tradition about the ways of the inner ancient self of cosmology, giving time to meditating as it is of a meditation, living in the third eye. Giving Isis giving to ones, fasting and giving thanks that InI soul should maintain redemption from the pessimistic vampires of colonial world that follows the ways of the dragon, the beast and the harlot walking after their own lust and having men's persons in admiration because of advantage.

At the time of *the rapture* - Nyahbinghì - within the gathering of InI self together to leave the wilderness region of the earth, Europe and America those are the wilderness placeless, remember that in Revelation 17: there where Yohanes said that he saw the harlot being carried by the beast, in verse 3' *so he carried me away in the spirit into the wilderness, that are the places where Rome world queendom great cities are.'*

St Luke chapter 17:v26-30,*'and as it was in the days of Noah, so shall it be also in the days of the son of man,- king Ras Tafari -, they did eat, they drank, they married wives, they were given in marriage, until the day that Noah entered into the ark, and the flood came and, destroyed them all. Likewise also as it was in the days of Lot, they did eat, they drank, they brought, they sold, they planted, they built, but the same day that Lot went out of Sodom it rained fire and brimstone from heaven, and destroyed them all, even thus shall it be in the day when the son of man is revealed.'*

The gathering gets near complete when ones gets the *overstanding* of Nyahbinghì faith that is *the rapture. The raptured* are taken away from world duties.

Right now InI are going through the book that is spoken of in Revelation chapter 5:v2 that Christ king Ras Tafari opened, Imajesty has loose the seven seals and the place where InI are at is the fifth seal.

InI are living through that portion' now' when all InI 'Rapture, Nyahbinghì', are gathered into one place in knowledge through the reincarnation. Then InI shall enter the times of the sixth seal, and live through that sixth seal, right now InI are still trodding through the fifth seal, 'putting on white robes,' even though Imajesty Haile Selassie the 1st has loosed these seven seals, and InI have recognised the personality of Christ in his kingly character.

These are times of the prophecy, it is not a song and dance, and it is not just to celebrate the great events of remembrance dates. It is a hola Ivocation, called through the Nyahbinghì order to administer *the rapture* faith.

InI pilgrimage - everyday life - to the Rastafari house there is no duality living for the world and saying loosely they are Nyahbinghì not of the world; they are wrong because people of the world do not have this Nyahbinghì faith.

The apostle Jude clearly explains that one's will know them, those are without InI Irits, knowledge, many whom spirit will faint in the presence of Nyahbinghì fire knowledge powers, the Irits has to be Ital without blood sacrifice when a one gives thanks to receive the hola visitation.

For in their duality they see another, they hear another, another speaks in their sensitive search they find another, they are another, truths are devotion to Imajesty

Christ in his kingly character Ras Tafari Makonnen as the supreme means of Icentration on Inl Ivine livity and not answering the call of the world. Giving your most to material sense, Nyahbinghì spirit can only be known through union with it, baptism into Nyahbinghì faith, *the rapture*.

Times of *the rapture* from Christ in his kingly character Ras Tafari has been identified and recognized. Fornication - mixing of seeds - is an abomination for the judgment that is unto the nations of Shem, Ham and Ja-pheth.

St Matthew chapter 25:v31-34, *'when the son of man shall come in his glory, and all the hola angels with him; then shall he sit upon the throne of his glory, and before him shall be gathered all nations; and he shall separate them one from another, as a shepherd dividth his sheep from the goats; and he shall set the sheep on his right hand, but the goats on the left, then shall the king say unto them on his right hand, come ye blessed of my father, inherit the kingdom prepared for you from the foundation of the world.'*

Inl know that I fathers kingdom is not in this world of the anti-Christ. All nations must separate keeping unto their own in the purpose of breeding. For interbreeding, seed mixing is going against the spiritual cosmic law; it is inequity, scientific craft.

A portion of marriage is man and woman becoming one flesh together, all nations must worship the one I AM that I AM. Ones can worship together, work and teach together, to live in earth as brothers and sisters.

Knowing that different nations have different blessings the blessings given unto Shem Ham and Japheth customs, nation quality's' therefore keeping the high spiritual laws of quality's from the blessings and curses given unto Shem, Ham and Japheth their nations inheritance forIver according to their works in earth and these nations are identified in genetic pigmentation.

Ones can see whose nation are administering Lucifer's nuclear destruction of the earth population of all races therefore nation quality's for the purpose of the creation master most high king Ras Tafari.

The evil mafiaism of those of "the camp David agreement "the modern world Sini covenant, purpose is to stop and prevent Inl from being a nation, see yourself being fleshly manifested in the Caribbean, sighted in a national material status, because the world teaches material concepts. "Where in political rights in truths is your nation? They are clearly fighting a spiritual war, separating in scattering then them turned anglophiles nationals causing internal tribal wars.

Within *the rapture* in the appearing of Christ in his kingly character Haile Selassie 1st the redeemer, separating from these nations is command *repatriation*. Nyahbinghì order has commands and also carries rebuke, that Inl rebuke those nations. Inl are not here to adopt the ways of the world, Lucifer's world of colonial values, slave masters mentality, any whose work is in maintaining colonial captivity, even the sweeper of the Roman roads of their glory. Worse is he that decorates their world, and furnishes tools of their appreciation.

InI pilgrimage is a hola trod, walking in a Mount Zion, Mount Zion is a hola place, a Binghì man cannot be on a money works every day, as if everything them do is for money, there is a time for everything.

Nyahbinghì is a tabernacle Icracy administration, it is an inbound knowledge of InI ancient tradition, it is not about works to the world, that way you're giving your worth to the beast. InI have works in the earth, yes in the Armageddon, which is the complete destruction of the world ways in earth. Cosmic rapture Nyahbinghì is as a Batawi towards the world.

Colonial values, observing worldly political patterns and laws, of false pretence, dualist claim the world and Nyahbinghì, what use is the Binghì to the one who does not know the spirit (Irits) of Nyahbinghì? What use is the rapture to those who are not within the gates, Zion gates that one enters only through fire baptism, 'brethren and sistren many a ones to the foundation all have to go down to the foundation, Nyahbinghì Tabernacle, that's the only way to enter here in Nyahbinghì administration.

Chapter Two

The Sini Covenant

Exodus 19-20.'Mount Sini in Ethiopia Camp David ancient dominion empire, Inl supreme authority.

Israel was sanctified from Egypt never to return therein.

The Camp David Agreements

The Sini covenant, Jimmy Carter of America with others of Rome, Europe and the rest of the world has brought again this modern day democracy Israel and Egypt together. They have formed a covenant, 'Sini Covenant' their treaty of 17th September 1978, which is a false covenant at a place in a gentile authority that is called 'Camp David', which is also false.

Camp David is Inl royal house Inl ancient dominion empire, of Haile Selassie the 1st. King David Camp' the black man of Shem Melchizedek camp and they made a covenant in that land of gentile authority that they are calling camp David on Mount Sini – Zion – without Inl Ethiopian/African Haile Selassie 1st, King David family. The black nation that are now at this time subjected to the Roman Jews and those who went with America Egypt and modern day democracy Israel.

Without the African in their Camp David agreement, every time that power is spoken of, they are claiming Haile Selassie 1st authority and power which they have not that power, neither the authority there. They are trying to annihilate the black man, especially the Rastafari and make out they are Inl all that is to stop Inl from being a nation.

Resistance

Against

Satanic

Teachings &

Annihilation

Inl sanctification – separation - from the world is now being in Ivine livity receiving Ivine cosmic radiance to ones Irits, carrying the Irits of the city's Mount Zion and Judah. There dwells the throne of the house of King David being in the presence of another realm that is not of Babylon queendom.

These cities are ways and customs of Inl supreme authority to be maintained in Irits Ituinually every step of Inl live. Following Christ in his kingly character Ras Tafari within *the rapture* Irits everything has been made renew, Inl reincarnation whilst in flesh alive on earth to the eyes of the world.

1st Samuel chapter 10:v6, *'and the spirit - Irits - of the lord will come upon thee, and thou shalt prophesy with them, and shalt be turned into another man; - reincarnation - those that are the living dead spiritually, they have only material sense spirit. From their mind they see 'reincarnation as having to have a new material manifestation, because to them their physical life is their foundation, although 'genesis chapter 1:v2 'and the spirit moved upon the waters.'*

Without the spirit of essence cosmic principles InI could not live Iternal.

The movement now Repatriation and Restoration separate and return to InI home land Ethiopia mother land Africa to wait until the time of restoration. The movement of repatriation is to separate from nations, Marcus Garvey's movement was to separate and inhabit a land of InI authority prepared for InI from the supreme architect the I AM that I AM.

As for InI of Rastafari way of live, InI main focus in earth is repatriation, away from the lands of Gentile authorities where the great evils live and the reaches of fornication, Ezra chapter 9:v2, *'for they have taken of their daughters for themselves, and their sons; so that the hola seed have mingled themselves with the people of those lands; ye, the hand of the princes and rulers hath been chief in this trespass.'*

2nd Corinthians chapter 6:v17, *'wherefore come out from among them, and be ye separate, saith the lord, and touch not the unclean thing; and I will receive you.'*

For sure fulfilment of the prophecies and the perseverance, livity of InI faith, it is essential to separate from the nations of Ham and Ja-pheth, when ones see the Binghi backslide in foreign lands it's because the trod that they are trodding has been distorted by artificial means of preservation that being the reason Christ in his kingly character Haile Selassie 1st, InI saviour has manifested in the flesh, that all eyes could of sighted HIM.

Genesis chapter 15:v13-14,*' and he said unto Abram, know of a surety, that thy seed shall be a stranger in a land that is not theirs, and shall be enslaved and they shall afflict them four hundred years, and also that nation, whom they shall serve will I judge; and afterwards shall they come out with great substance.'*
Spiritual material and money goes hand in hand, one does not go without the other as InI are passing through earth, but InI shall only love the spiritual and creation material in its natural state.

There is time of times in *the rapture* that is revealed in Revelation that InI must acknowledge whether they are visible or unseen, InI must carry in Irits, InI faith that has been handed down InI great ancient cities of knowledge, ones must know Nyahbinghi faith.

It is knowledge in *the rapture* of Christ in his kingly character, truths prepared for InI by the supreme architect of heaven and earth. In the time of *the rapture* reincarnation Nyahbinghi InI with Christ Ras Tafari in his kingly character, twelve kings 'the twelve apostles, shall reincarnate within Rastafari livity, as spoken of in Matthew chapter 19:v27-28, *'then answered Peter and said unto him, behold, we have forsaken all, and followed thee; what shall we have therefore? and Christ said unto them, verily I say unto you that ye which have followed me, in the regeneration when the son of man shall sit in the throne of his glory, ye also shall sit upon twelve thrones, judging the twelve tribes of Israel.'*

These thrones are of InI supreme authority of InI Dominion Empire those are in InI heavens InI must find them *iritcally*. Nyahbinghì children it's crucial, imperative to live in the administration function powers of InI faith, as King Ras Tafari Makonnen has removed himself from the sight of man and people.

InI must walk now closer in the Nyahbinghì administration Nyahbinghì I. King Ras Tafari live foriver. InI are in the presence of unseen forces, in truths one must take strength and don't let the weakness live. Live up in InI faith strength forward for InI pilgrimage is to the Rastafari house, either visible or invisible. It is vital ones must carry the knowledge of Nyahbinghì faith *the rapture*.

Colossians chapter 1:v15-16, *'who is the image of the invisible god, the first born of every creature. For by him were all things created that are in heaven and that are in earth, visible and invisible, whether they be thrones, or dominions, or principalities, or powers; all things were created by him, and for him.'*

Many brethren of the Nyahbinghì carry a teaching that says that the early elders, - the patriarchs - *did not deal with the New Testament.*

Marcus Garvey, who first interpreted a portion of the prophecy, looked forward to Africa – Ethiopia - for the crowing of the king of kings, 'he shall be the redeemer, and a great portion of Marcus Garvey's interpretations came from the New Testament.

The teachings of the Second Advent of Christ in his kingly character, Haile Selassie 1st again the greater portion is revealed in the New Testament. There are those in the wilderness of the world that say that the earlier elders only dealt with Revelations.

That also is wrong, a contradiction of the truth, distorting the teachings of Nyahbinghì faith in *the rapture* of Christ in his kingly character Ras Tafari. Worse are those that say that 'Nyahbinghì is known as the pinnacle, ' if that reference is to the pinnacle of the 'St Matthew chapter 4:v5, *'then the devil taketh him up in to the holy city and setteth him on a high point of the temple.'*

At that high point the devil could manifest there, all that could be achieved there were the kingdoms of the world. That wasn't hola Mount Zion, where InI dwell in InI heavenly assembly in cosmology of earth a place called Zion in Ethiopia Camp David ancient dominion empire there no evil can make manifestation.

The pinnacle as a high Mountain place in earth is a worldly thing, that couldn't be known as Nyahbinghì, because InI faith is not of the world. Nyahbinghì truth is unquestionably *the rapture*.

The need to interpret Nyahbinghì faith, *the rapture* so that the world could recognize and have an *overstanding* of InI Ivine faith that is a love, relating to the prophecy of

this love Christ in his kingly character Haile Selassie 1st and the myriads of Ingels, InI Nyahbinghi administration in *the rapture*.
There is also the word Elder and the over standing of the Elderly, an elder is not just one who is old in age; 'an elder or the elderly is an elder in knowledge of the rapture Nyahbinghi faith.' They are the fullness of Rastafari way of life, one who carries the ancient cities in knowledge of InI cosmic tradition.

The elderly is the most knowledgeable in an Igregration – congregation – 'high priest, prince, prophet in the tabernacle in the cities of InI irits, InI receive daily visitation. Many Elderly says that all the Ible 'prophecy is true and InI knows that too, yet it is imperative that InI must only know how to interpret the prophecy that is written there.

As for those who say that they are not dealing with the New Testament, know that 'one of the founders of the H.Y.B.F (house of the youth black faith) carried the Nyahbinghi theocracy order in its infancy. He carried the torch all the days of his Nyahbinghi administrative pilgrimage visible earthly trod a miracle of InI faith, Ras Boanerges (Bongo Watu) a miracle and fire Ingel of *the rapture*.

Ras Boanerges name came from the New Testament meaning 'son of thunder' St Mark chapter 3:v17, *'And the son of Zebedee, and John the brother of James; and he surnamed them Boanerges, which is' the sons of thunder.'*

Ras Boanerges InI elderly brethren, patriot surely accepted the teachings of the New Testament and not just Revelation, the gospel and the letters to the Igregration at that time, more so for the 'Rapture' InI faith. The New Testament is vital for the Revelation of Christ in his kingly character Haile Selassie 1st the returned messiah King Ras Tafari.

2nd Thessalonians chapter 1:v7-8,*'and to you who are troubled rest with us, when the Lord Christ shall be revealed from heaven with his mighty ingels, in flaming fire taking vengeance on them that know not god and that obey not the gospel of our lord I Negus I Christ.'*

Also in Revelation chapter 3:v12, 'I will write upon him my new name,
Revelation reveals to InI that Haile Selassie 1st is the Christ King and in the rapture he shall have a new name.
1st Thessalonians chapter 4:v16-17,*'for the lord himself shall 'lasend from heaven with a shout, with the voice of the archangel, and with the trumpet of god; and the dead in Christ shall rise first, then we which are alive and remain shall be caught up together with them in the clouds, to meet the lord in the air; and so shall we ever be with the lord.'*

I Negus I Christ say's I am the resurrection.

Chapter Three

The Rapture: Cosmic Tradition

InI tradition is a cosmic mystical journey only can be taught from those who are in that tradition the ways of the inner itself, the administration 'given' introduced at the time of entering baptism into InI faith it's an Ital Irits and no alcoholism 'not giving thanks to blood sacrifice, - therefore no flesh, no wine, rum or stout mouth can speak from a Ital consciousness - it is impossible.

When one leaves behind the world and trod forward into Zion gates, where all natural gifts, powers are from self Itrol as the highest supreme architect will not give unto a one more than one can handle.

Meditating on the soul spirit within, without including anything of the world, that is destined to change or dissolve InI spirit becomes a sacrifice, ones sacrifice becomes sacred (dedicated) to the divine supreme architect, a life of self-control and disinterested ego action is a sacrifice.

The all-seeing lord the "I AM that I AM" of Ethiopia sit upon the rainbow royal throne in judgement, knowing InI inner battle maintaining Icentration on the higher sense's and rejecting the material senses concepts that our fullness is of birth and death. For InI faith there is no beginning or end, I cosmic spirit being long before creation and the world the spirit supreme everlasting.

The material sense comes not from the spirit but from earthly/ worldly delusion when ones live for the material, those who live for the world of masters who design, organize and provide things for their fame and personal powers and thus become their guide/leader. There you go idol worshiping 'giving thanks to things that represent confusion from egoistic demons that are not Iternal.

The soul, the spirit of I which is the focus of the I AM that I AM in all, that focus has a free will came into the world in the material body of a baby dominated by the collective wills of the world, leaders and peoples of dogmatic lives. InI the keepers of truths and rights, followers of Christ in his kingly character, has to be reincarnated when the flesh is ripen as to the sacred Ivine will of the I AM (God), in sanctification separation from the will of the world, there is the soul that is never reincarnated to the Ivine living of the supreme architect, that soul is bound by the pleasures of material nature composed of the elements of the body.

Iditation to master the knowledge for the knowledge is the strength that gives self-control to rule ones Irits mind against the flow of the world and outside of Zion influence, keeping ones thought in the present administration livity, living InI ancient way in this modern times and not in the past, yesterday or in the future where you may not reach in the same form.

Many self-styled Rastafarians have no knowledge are without Nyahbinghi Irits those will never be able to recognise InI administration of the inner I, knowing only worldly ways, ceremonies, rituals and prays without knowledge of inner self kingdom from within administration. The inner is provided by essence cosmic principles every universal elements, knowing Haile Selassie the 1st creation of galaxies, Imajesty Ras Tafari as real in the world as within, inner reality(powers of I AM).

The preachers of the churches of the world today, they teach of *the rapture* superficially as for example 'there will be no disappearance (vanishing) of any large amount of people or any physical flesh and blood meeting on the clouds all these are wrong interpretations to confuse the truth all the talk about pre-rapture is nonsense.

The rapture can only be correct that which include Christ in his kingly character and the Ingels all who trod the earth, having material of blood, flesh and bones, whilst on earth. Also having an inner cosmic spiritual form, that can be visible when outside of one's earthly material body. InI cosmic form flies and excels at tremendous speed. InI cosmic image of InI earthly form does enter the above kingdom of the supreme architect or even hades if that is ones pay.

Of the 'Rapture' What there will be, from the second appearance of I Negus I Christ in his kingly character Ras Tafari Imajesty the king of kings, the Ivine black messiah elect of god, recognize head of InI Nyahbinghi *the rapture*, a great number of people will renounce the world. Taking leave of their worldly occupations abandoning social duties, dismissing worldly family ties rejecting worldly professionalism and declaring the messiah Christ in his kingly character Haile Selassie the 1st, the root of David, two hundred and twenty fifth in the lineage of King Solomon manifested in the land of Ethiopia. InI material is the true seed of the Jew, the royal Jew of Jerusalem, and throne in Ethiopia today.

Whatever age in time ones sight up that,' it's never too late, because the truth shall remain forIver, as Imajesty Christ in his kingly character Haile Selassie the 1st glory shall forIver grow Iternal without end.

They will catch up in their heavenly glory and meet Christ in his kingly character and InI Nyahbinghi *the rapture* in the air' that InI breath, because that is the key 'the precious breath of life' the air is cosmic the tradition is cosmic, in the clouds, the clouds is strength cosmic strength InI know that heaven of cosmology is above, (until that kingdom comes on earth).

The worldly focus is purely earthbound, fortune, fame, associates, InI earthly body is from the earth and for the earth, InI soul-spirit is from above in the cosmic InI spiritual journey away from the earth, takes InI ascending through the clouds, riding the wings of the wind higher cosmic trod is above' in time' between the air, clouds sky, in galaxy infinity.

InI greatest acknowledgement of InI lord Ras Tafari shall be away from the earth, in the air through the winds of clouds which begins the gate way of cosmic heaven above.

It is difficult for a material sense man of the world, who lives on a purely material plane, and only accept what he sees to know the Ivine essence cosmic principle powers, that are not known, 'seen' through a worldlians senses. The power of illusion the thought of action that isn't real, not correct. The earthly foe the enemy of hola soul makes the world appear real, pleasures and sufferings binds persons to worldly existence whereas the Iniversal essence (soul) is the ultimate reality. It is indestructible and InI invisible focus that requires time and Iditation on InI ancient cities rebuilding those cities irits in ones heavens of InI ancient Dominion Empire of supreme authority the essence cosmic principle powers that is life forIver.

Ones must give their most to search in their Irits heavens and find those king wise cities and carry them; they are greater than the king/queendom of Babylon empires. InI embodiment still not separate from InI visible form, whilst occupying the material, Haile Selassie the 1st supremacy visible also invisible, Christ in his kingly character Haile Selassie the 1st is now and forIver.

2 Corinthians, 5:v1, *'for we know that if our earthly house of this tabernacle were dissolved, we have a building of god a house not made with hands, eternal in the heavens.'*

The rapture Irits is the essence of Nyahbinghì faith, the inner I that worldlians have never seen, the ever living I whose presence ones have felt: I object (image) is all of this world earth.

The rapture of Christ in his kingly character, *'the rapture* is a time of judgment, it is the resurrection, for *I Negus I* Christ said in St John 11: v 25, *' I am the resurrection' and the life, he that believeth in me, though he 'were dead' yet shall he live.'*

The rapture InI faith the spirit (soul) given to InI, that is amongst the things of the world and yet is above the things of this world. That it must be beyond the life of the material body and the mind, 'never born and never dying (without beginning and without ending) ever living, the invisible force making an exchange in the body dissolving the weak and restoring the strong and powerful. Without the living spirit of soul, through reincarnation, resurrection of the cosmos, the essence of the embodiment is worldly dead of principle.

Revelation 20:v4-5, *'they came to life and reigned with Christ a thousand years, but the rest of the dead lived not again until the thousand years were finished.'*

Ras Tafari live so InI *the rapture* 'all those that came in *the rapture* that have had the fire baptism, been reincarnated shall live with Imajesty Haile Selassie the 1st, in the millennium not as millenniumists, but as *the rapture*, a faith that shall be recognise by the world, at the declaring of Christ in his second advent the returned messiah the Christ in his kingly character, Haile Selassie the 1st imajesty Ras Tafari art the returned I Negus I Christ and InI in that faith Nyahbinghì are *the rapture*.

The nations have stolen all that belongeth to InI nation, they have claimed all InI inheritance, even camp David is in America, and the 1st Haile Selassie in Ethiopia is king David great, great, great, great and great grandson, 225th they cannot claim I rapture because they haven't accepted the return of Christ in his kingly character, they know of *the rapture* from the prophecy but they don't know Nyahbinghì in the prophecy.

In America they are making a big fuss today about *the rapture*, their scientific confusion, trying to tire out the people in Babylon mysteries hoping for a majority go with the flow pattern thing, it won't work forever, but during Christ in his kingly character Ras Tafari first thousand years, the world will have the larger portion of people spell bound with the sting of the world, hiding behind dead presidents working for dead presidents.

Note the anti-Christ appeared in the world as a president, therefore the seat of the president is the seat of the anti-Christ, and following false prophets. There is no reincarnation in the reggae house, there is no Ivine livity in the reggae house, there is Ras Tafari name in reggae music, but there isn't a single element in practice of InI faith in that music.

That's why the way of life of the Nyahbinghì administration is not the same way as those that carry the sting of the world. InI live to reincarnate InI original way of live, Ivine livity restoring the ancient cities, where there is every day Ivine visitation.

Reincarnation of the dead the world was dead when I Negus I Christ came in to the world, from the foundation of the world transgressors who chose object sense guide than the eyes and guidance of the father, many wanted to be a separate from the' I AM that I AM'.

There was only one other who was reincarnated unto Ivinity that was Shem Melchezedek although he was manifested of flesh of sin. I Negus I Christ was manifested a hola flesh and Ivine spirit (Irits) the first born of the dead.

Colossians 1:v17-18 *'he is before all things, and in him all things hold together, and he is the head of the body, the church, he is the beginning and the first born from among the dead.'*

Ever living 'the world brought their most powerful concept of death upon him and he conquered death, because he lives forever, whether invisible or visible the illusion of death is not a reality because when the maker of heaven and earth first created the body from the dust of the earth, it did not live until the "life" precious breath was blown into it. That's undeniable proof that the material is not the life, the material makes a life in the world/earth, but life is the gift to the material body, the life's breath (essence of cosmic principles) which has no end, the concepts of the world tries to drown the essence of cosmic principles with the ways of the world, that has been so long a burden to man and woman because of their intellect.

Nyahbinghì *the rapture* carrying the last trumpet which is the first reincarnation of (those) the dead in I Negus I Christ: manifest forward conquering death with Christ in his kingly character Haile Selassie the 1st king of kings & lord of lords.

1 Thessalonians 4:v16-17 *'for the lord himself will come down from heaven, with a loud command, with the voice of the archangel and with the trumpet call of (god) and the dead in Christ will rise first, after that, we who are still alive and are left will be caught up together with them in the clouds to meet the lord in the air, and so we will be with the lord forever.'*

That is how who were the dead in Christ are reincarnated in *the rapture* with Christ in his kingly character, these are *the rapture* the Ingels/ saints Nyahbinghì, giving the shout and living Iternal with and for Christ in his kingly character Ras Tafari Haile Selassie 1st.

But the worldly, the intellects of the world who put their worldly occupation and the will of other men before the will of Christ in his kingly character Haile Selassie 1st, masters hold them in advantage by paying them a wage, they who robbed and murdered to heap up for themselves and their kins, the precious metals, stones and stole the wealth of the earth.

Today those hypocrite nations look upon Africa/Ethiopia in scorn or with pretence and continue in their mocking, those worldlians or so called followers of the anti-Christ, when they receive in their hearts true justice and love of the Christ in his kingly character of Ethiopia and not the Roman worship the one in the of picture Michael Angelo's painting, turning I Negus I the black Nazarene into a gentile then they will catch up with Inl *the rapture*.

It is true that those of the churches of the world those who have to live according to the gospel until they proclaim that I Negus I Christ in his kingly character has returned according to his promise in the book of John chapter 14:v3, *'and if I go and prepare a place for you, I will come again and receive you unto myself; that where I am, there ye may be also.'*

Then any one able to enter the livity of Revelation where the ways of I Negus I Christ is not the same as the gospel, where he has come as the greatest king of kings in judgement and not turn the other cheek.

2 Corinthians 5:v7, *'we live by faith not by sight, we are confident I say and would prefer to be away from the body and at home with the lord.'*

Faith embodies visible reality and things not seen, things not seen by reason of material sense as by the eyes of the body, but seen by the spirit in the third eye, even though we know that Inl do not have to visibly see Haile Selassie the 1st because Inl saviour is forIver with Inl'.

Romans1:v20, *'for since the creation of the world god's invisible qualities- his eternal power and divine nature, have been clearly seen, being understood from what has been made, so that men are without excuse.'*

Here on earth spiritual, material and money these go hand in hand, they all together are not one thing; when one ceases (as the body) or money another can continue, and that which is eternal shall forever be, when Inl work shall be done on this earth Inl inner union with truths is beyond the world of the body, the ways of the world i.e. tools of the world (professionalism) none of the ways of the world is required for the soul livity, the soul spirit is not earth bound, does not have a kingdom in earth until the fulfilment of Revelation, earth is a material heaven a place where the six sense feast in temporal pleasures.

The sun, the moon the universe and every interdependent thing in the cosmic within InI, as from extravert to introvert, the inner manifestations of I inner cosmic tradition is always at that moment "now" the present, so whilst one's busy sorting the world, they are dead to it, (unconscious) of the ever living I.

Luke 17:v20, 'the kingdom of god does not come with your careful observation, nor will people say,' here it is' because the kingdom of god is within you.'

Then again in John 18:v36,'I Negus I Christ said "my kingdom is not of this world, if it were my servants would fight to prevent my arrest by the Jews 'but now my kingdom is from another place, the kingdom of the maker of heaven and earth.'

In fact is within, because that is the only place, where all the creation past, present and future can be attained, stored, replaced or renewed and remain eternal. Gathered in thought preserved in word, built in remembrance, grow in spirit Irits that is also why I Negus I Christ said, 'heaven and earth shall pass away but my words shall remain, kept in knowledge, essence cosmic principles.'

Learn to meditate in knowledge of InI precious Ivine breath of life that InI breath to see another day in the 3rd eye, search out InI administration Nyahbinghì faith, Rastafarian way of life in Iditation knowledge and when all the worldly desires that cling to the heart fade out then the material addiction becomes spiritual love.

Then true identity in this life attains redemption road from the world, reincarnation is redemption from of the world. There are no truths in the world, only superficial facts which are all transcended when searched out.

The way to Mount Zion 'the highest region of InI faith is to love Imajesty Christ in his kingly character Ras Tafari with all your heart and soul, not just with your mind or through the perfecting of ritual observances, InI way is a road where Ingels trod, many of Ingels in one administration, it's what the administrators ones around the altar can make manifest Iritcally.

In addition to powers of movements through word sound and powers, everything is brought into the presence of the most high Haile Selassie the 1st, the administration functions from the Nyahbinghì tabernacle around the altar, 'the prescribed place' whatever is administered there. This is what goes up into the cosmic as the administering Ingels ride up in the cosmic heavens and carry forward deliver InI presentations testimonies that will go into all the earth and cosmic affecting all.

The will of the supreme architect shall work because the tabernacle is in the realm of authority. Irusalam/Zion cosmic authority, Ivine authority, Haile Selassie the 1st is InI light, the light that allows InI rapture to administer Nyahbinghì, know and see InI celestial spiritual body, that InI can ride upon the wings of the wind.

InI faith is claimed firm in the New Testament for I Negus I Christ Imessiah in that advent is family of king David and Solomon, yet it is through Imajesty Christ in his kingly character Ras Tafari InI faith *the rapture* is structured, and the New Testament is livicated to (the) times of Christ Imajesty Haile Selassie 1st past, present and future infinite Nyahbinghì I rapture I.

The rapture are those of the Nyahbinghi that are written about in the prophecy with Christ in his kingly character Haile Selassie the 1st in Mount Zion cosmology and Ethiopia earth.

Chapter Four

Nyahbinghì: Mount Zion

The rapture faith Nyahbinghì administration is not about man and women, personal issue's Nyahbinghì is a tabernacle Icracy administration. The Nyahbinghì is not a person, the Nyahbinghì is an administration, it is an authority on the administration and InI are the tabernacle Icracy administration of the tabernacle church of the highest Christ in his kingly character Janhoy Ras Tafari.

InI are the Ingels administering through InI tabernacle Icracical administration Imajesty Christ in his kingly character Haile Selassie the 1st living church, a heavenly assembly passing through earth, the tabernacle administration is about pleasing serving the supreme architect, not men and peoples, Nyahbinghì is a title bestowed on a one at baptism. Without the fire baptism that title one cannot have, one has to enter through the tabernacle receiving decorations to have any authority in InI livity.

One heart one black love, black love is not the colour of a ones skin, black is the colour of Ivinity the life is a Ivine love therefore it is a black love, one Haile Selassie the 1st, one Nyahbinghì order, the administration is one, one effect, no personal effect, does not administer personal issues, personal issues are not included in *the rapture* personal is outside of InI administration.

Imajesty Haile Selassie the 1st has already prepared InI live, any personal life is about man and woman, the administration is not a personal thing, should any individual take it personal,' they are not knowing neither seeing the administration, personal is ego 'self-serving', wanting Haile Selassie the 1st for themselves.

The administration is an order, 'that does not tarry with personal affairs personal is not Nyahbinghì, the personal is of the world, no woman belongs to no man, you cannot administrate Nyahbinghì on account of your woman or children. Remember Abram was about to sacrifice Isaac, it is not a personal thing although InI are individuals, Nyahbinghì carries commands, as InI know no man can save no man Nyahbinghì is not about them.

Nyahbinghì administration is administering the cosmic order and preserving InI ancient cities Irits; Nyahbinghì is all about *the rapture* of Christ in his kingly character in Ivine administration. All thanks and glories are to the maker of heaven and earth Christ in his kingly character Haile Selassie the 1st.

Nyahbinghì administration *'the rapture'* is of a cosmic Issembly, it is not compatible with the ways of the world, it is not comprehensive to the living of the world, it is a portion that has not been told, the ancient Ethiopian way of life, not known to the world, weak heart cannot know it, because death is a barrier.

Death is the concept of a weak heart who cannot transcend the theories of the world concepts that hold them in the region of the living dead, those are they who give their all for the world and do not value their soul, that they gave it through want, then their heart desires are gained and their soul goes to the giver and the one who deceived the world, the deceiver of the world, because the world has been deceived and I Negus I Christ was crucified from the foundation of the world. The order of the supreme architect cannot be decided because of man and woman, but the Nyahbinghì theocracy tabernacle administration is all about adoring Christ in his kingly character Imajesty Haile Selassie the 1st.

The world leaders distribute the illusion and ones thinking that one's have a personal life, but it's the way of the world captivity bounded in colonial values, though hola is the life, I Negus I Christ is the life and the way, he is hola (holy), InI have to follow Christ in his kingly character Ras Tafari because InI came with him in *the rapture* known in the world as Nyahbinghì and no one else.

InI existence is on earth at this time but InI citizenship is in heaven cosmology galaxy, hola Mount Zion is InI home the Rastafari house. When the material body cease to function on earth, the soul spirit the celestial body has left and continues to live through the cosmic in Mount Zion. InI ever living Irits are essence cosmic principles, the essence you cannot see, you cannot grab hold of I because all material is of the world on earth.

They are subject to change and dissolvent and what is of the world is not the Iternal I, in truths I am what you cannot see, I am reflected through I object form of sense, as the essence of action after the action can you get the essence, as you cannot touch the inner I now' how much less so after I trod through.

There is essence in all action,' the essence you cannot see, sight InI essence' can you steal my soul? My heavenly treasure the true I? Do you know my Irits? Can you direct my cosmic radiance? Ones can only compare with them if you are of them, Rastafari is a love, to know InI love you must know the inner galaxy, the inner universe of all elements unseen forces invisible not of the world, then you will know InI *rapture* for consciousness is the source of the universe.

Those who seek to move InI heavens, or steal I soul, they are dead, those have never lived, they will have to reach every interdependent essence (elements) every interbeing, fire will burn them, go first to the sun and wait there for I.

InI way of life cannot be reached by conceptual knowledge or in the categories of mental discrimination, InI are not bound or restrained by the elements no one can take away the Binghì, Imajesty Haile Selassie 1st and the truths in InI, the whole of I heart is Nyahbinghì. For one has to be Nyahbinghì first before Rastafari, because Haile Selassie the 1st, he only is Rastafari. InI live forever in *the rapture*, birth and death cannot touch I as InI have never been born and I will never die, birth did not give I existence, neither does material death take away existence, I am I Irits, but not the object senses of the world, I am the invisible cosmic radiance that allowed the body to live, have life at the creation of Adam and Eve.

Ivinity life must not be recognise through action and visible material purely at this time, because the action or material might not be of your way of life but are there to be adopted, because InI know that every material substance in earth is subject to change, 'though the gift of God is eternal life, and eternal is infinite, the living I in Zion in heaven "away from earth" is not an earthly material place, but it is a celestial material a place of radiance, that is visible and invisible but yet cannot change and cannot dissolve, earthly material cannot enter there.

Should any earthly object form start that journey, it shall reach there in a celestial form, should that be its place of abode ones cannot reach there with money, or machines nor skin, flesh, bone and beauty, but Mount Zion beauty is as the rainbow and I celestial beings are jewels perfect in (their) wonder as the stars are in the skies.

Mount Zion is forIver eternal, infinite, also those on earth who are from Mount Zion heavenly Issembly, InI that came in *the rapture* to reincarnate Nyahbinghì even on earth InI are Mount Zion, so is InI strong hold dwelling place Ethiopia, but InI Iternal home office is in heavens in the cosmology galaxies.

In truths heavenly Mount Zion cannot be comprehended to the fullness by InI, so leave not everything to your own overstanding. Only Ras Tafari the head creator is the master the actor and orator, Nyahbinghì is not God, do not compare one's self with Haile Selassie the 1st, though one of the terms for Nyahbinghì is, *she that possess many things*, many things not everything.

Self-control and living in meditation in the 3rd eye on InI administration away from the world is two of the greatest aspects of Rastafari livity, mastering mind and emotions, actions must be carried out without worldly desires or attachment to the outcome, so that InI can engage in the world but not be controlled by it.

At the resurrection the renewing of all things the mystical rapture return of Christ in his kingly character is the resurrection time, Imajesty with InI Ingels Nyahbinghì shall all live at the resurrection, returning forward to the light and hola life of Christ in his kingly character, forgetting the world and the ways of the world =(Rome).

The resurrection is the condition of those who have risen in reincarnation from the dead born in sin world, reincarnated with the forgiveness of all sins not to remember the ways of the world, and having a sacred significance that is beyond human understanding, a knowledge of reality beyond the understanding of material senses. Incarnation of Nyahbinghì, means that he who is Ingel comes into the earth world as man in flesh, the resurrection and reincarnation (born of the dead) are two in the same thing to 'renew'.

Although some people think of them as strictly physical matters, which can also include the physical, ones think also of a collective mass of people all at the same moment, that is not so because it is a gathering, a reincarnation of the dead.

The Rapture and the resurrection spoken of by I Negus I Christ' told of himself as the resurrection, to his apostles whilst he was with them, now that Christ in his kingly character Haile Selassie the 1st are with InI forIver 'so that where he is InI are' InI are in the resurrection time, that he had spoken of, a time of renewing a time of gathering, and a time of judgement every day *until* Christ in his kingly character Haile Selassie the 1st kingdom comes upon the earth as it is in heaven - the fulfilment, the new Irusalem comes to earth in the land of the ark of the covenant Ethiopia.

Why are they running away from king Ras Tafari, St Luke 20:v34-36, *'and Christ answering said unto them, the children of this world marry, and are given in marriage; but they which shall be accounted worthy to obtain that world, and the resurrection from the dead, neither marry, nor given in marriage; nether can they die anymore; for they are equal unto the Ingels; and are the children of god, being the children of the resurrection.'*

Furthermore Revelations reveals that the conquering lion stood in Mount Zion and with him a hundred forty and four thousand sealed, "having his father's name written in their foreheads.

Revelations 14:v4,*'these are they which were not defiled with woman: for they are virgins, these are they which follow the lamb whithersoever he goeth, these were redeemed from among men, being the first fruits unto god and the lamb.'*

Living together with a woman is marriage, and the 144,000 are of the tribe of Israel, InI also know of the organization called the 12 tribes of Israel, prophecy says that these virgins are of the tribes of Israel, InI Nyahbinghi *the rapture* chant songs that InI are the chosen few, InI Ingels are the escapees of Israel, InI trod Mount Zion, InI are Mount Zion, it is InI indwelling city, Isaiah 4:v2, *'in that day shall the branch of the lord be beautiful and glorious, and the fruit of the earth shall be excellent and comely for them that are escaped of Israel.'*

InI *the rapture* are not Israel, in InI Ivine livity there is authority in InI way of life through Nyahbinghi administration, that authority is received only through the tabernacle at the time of fire baptism and decorations. When you see a one who has entered this life through the tabernacle and has been decorated, know that she/he has authority and shall administer every step of their pilgrimage in authority.

Now with authority I write for those who are not of the world and are walking in Nyahbinghi administration in Zion Ethiopia Camp David, InI have come in *the rapture* with Christ in his kingly character Kadamawe Haile Selassie. The institution of marriage is the contract of the world, when ones signs that contract they are in agreement with that controlling policy the marriage of scientific knowledge and industry.

When two get married' in the western world' two become of the world (it may not be the same all around the earth) as InI know traditionally marriage is living together but in the so called modern world marriage is an institution,' that is a systematic science formed into a pattern for social control, using behaviour towards worldly principles, instead of sacred family love union, the institution manufactured by scientist experiments on passions, the ways of acting, thinking and feelings general in the system in social interaction subject to constraints or social regulations.

The already established customs and practices, relating to a particular science done in a systematic way from experiments and tests, marriage of the world belongs to scientists, scientists are their heads, they have manufactured a worldly enterprise.

Brethren must Ideate, search their heavens to think about these things deeply high to reflect on what holds them in the world, in Roman Babylon, and what are spiritual truths, for they have chosen lust for the whorehouse administration rather than Ingelic honour.

Those who think that the way to Mount Zion is through a woman's vagina, their love for the pleasures of the world and its vanity ways has denied themselves heavenly Issembly.

Reincarnation into *the rapture* the entry in to Mount Zion gate, is through the tabernacle Hebrews 12:v22, *'but ye are come unto Mount Zion, and unto the city of the living god, the heavenly Jerusalem, and to an innumerable company of angles, to the general assembly and church of the firstborn, which are written in heaven, and to god the judge of all, and to the spirits of just men made perfect.'*

Attendant values of love and duty, Nyahbinghì order (duty) to Mount Zion, Ethiopia sovereignty Icracy reign, InI *the rapture* (Nyahbinghì) has chosen eternal love, rather than mere worldly power.

In the time of *the rapture* the heavens that are attributed to the earth atmosphere, though beings seen and unseen elements shall be burned up, i.e. 'principles that have been infected.'

When one sees the Nyahbinghì administration backslide in places because Imajesty Haile Selassie the 1st has left the house visibly (earth), to Nyahbinghì administration, it is because of those that did not come into the Nyahbinghì faith through baptism in the tabernacle, they are the cause of the Binghì backslide.

The administrators who don't have the spirit Irits of Nyahbinghì 'knowledge'(self-appointed spoke persons) drivers trying to build InI way of life into the world, not knowing the drive of the administration, the faith, they form an organization trying to show InI compatible with the world ways.

Ones cannot administer Nyahbinghì through an organization, neither could Nyahbinghì be administered through a musical entertainment, the administration is the faith that is not an organization neither a musical.

The elements of one's Iritcally heaven are burned up, similarly people of the world when they exploit and damage the earth, plants and animals, natural resources, polluting the spirit of the earth, that the earth cannot produce what was intended at its beginning, then the earth will be laid bare.

2nd Peter 3:v1o-11, *'but the day of the Lord will come as a thief in the night; in the which the heavens shall pass away with a great noise, and the elements shall melt with a fervent heat, the earth also and the works that are therein shall be burned up, seeing then that all these things shall be dissolved, what manner of persons ought ye to be in all holy conversation and godliness.'*

In the time of InI rapture, gathering and awaiting restoration, the Revelations will be fulfilled, 2nd Peter 3:v13, *'nevertheless we, according to his promise, look for new heavens and a new earth, wherein dwelleth righteousness.'*

InI the essence cosmic principles 'the Irits' are what gives life to InI material form and that is the source of the inbound, so as the separate living material living objects, separate from own earthly form, gets cosmic attention,(service) and when they become inner I, it is their cosmic effects that joins InI inner cosmic principles. These are new heavens, all of the New Irusalem, that furnishes InI and gives the earth a new spirit that has always been in Mount Zion Issembly, but unknown and unseen to the worldly material sense (mortal), whose thoughts are that mother earth and all her material products.

Things that contained a soul or things without soul, was just to be used, and never even gave thanks for what they took pleasure in, those who thought the earth was only soil, never looked transcended further to see that the earth is living, giving birth to all material, as everything that lives must have a soul/spirit.

The fullness of the meaning of 2nd Peter 3:v9-14 is inbound and spiritual (Iritcally) that affects the outer world and universes, note carefully verse 11 shows InI must endure the judgement and sentence which is already hanging over all. Now in good will InI must harbour within *the rapture* the Nyahbinghi administration, these ways are for all Rastafari way of life nominations when those catch up to the fullness of 'Nyahbinghi' and know *the rapture*.

InI are the heavenly Issembly any others that have not reach the fullness,(have not received Ivinity) who are not *the rapture* until they catch up, nominations are traditions, the nominations Nyahbinghi, Ethiopian orthodox, Bobo Ashanty,12 tribes of Israel these four are traditions.

The realities is that the majority of Rastafarians fall short of the knowledge of the faith in *the rapture* of Christ in his kingly character and are splinters in their faith, as many have stopped at the reggae house in Israel where there is no reincarnation in the reggae house dance.

They have not the spirit(Irits) of Nyahbinghi, the splinter faith without knowledge of InI fullness, have developed mental states (mental illnesses) from the world, according to their mentality, which are the sources of sufferings, the reggae fuel food for thought administration is a splinter taken from InI faith.

Ivine livity, divine incarnate living the inbound truths way to live Rastafari way of life it's a love. I Negus I Christ is not of the world, there is no peace in the world, the world is not a place of love, the earth is also of the universes galaxies, the universes is a love, the world is not the truths and light of the living Christ in his kingly character Imajesty is ever at work, many are deluded if they think 'that these realities can be held up, the way and knowledge of *the rapture* is to furnish ones with heavens (knowledge) give fresh courage, inspiration, heart, soul and strength, into ones that the knowledge will live, with visions of the higher reality, to renew many a ones minds.

InI have been reincarnated through Christ in his kingly character imajesty Haile Selassie the 1st, and now myself of the world no longer live, but Christ in his kingly character King Ras Tafari live in InI, the life InI live in the body, I live by faith Nyahbinghì faith in the father, the son the hola one of creation, the power of the hola trinity, the all in one supreme architect ever living, I am nothing of myself- personal, as taught to I by the teachings of the world.

In the twinkle of an eye the hola one (spirit) will take hold, not through reading a book or ceremonies or rituals, but through the grace blessings of reincarnation baptism in Nyahbinghì tabernacle and power of Christ in his kingly character the one and only Haile Selassie the 1st Imajesty worketh through InI Nyahbinghì, *the rapture* InI Nyahbinghì Ivine livity has no beginning or ending, it is indescribable, in a context it is visible and invisible.

It is in the universe and the universe is in it, only in Imajesty Haile Selassie 1st can it be known in all. Ivine love is Imajesty Ras Tafari Makonnen and his blessings are given to Nyahbinghì *the rapture* in sanctifying InI from the world.

When InI cast away the bondage of the world, InI cast away the thought of works in the world is the way to Mount Zion, the works for the world are the bondage of the world, those whom are looking for material merits seeking recognition through events established in the world, fire burn them , they are without the spirit of Nyahbinghì.

Those shall faint in heart as they face the fire of judgment, they bow to the world to save their material life and hope in vain that the world take not their goods, world honour, children or wife or the world should allow and promote them to have those things, yet these profits are small, all 'these things shall vanish then the city (Ivine livity) of the 'I AM that I AM' will be all that remaineth.

Chapter Five

Melchizedek Intrusion

The earliest mention of reincarnation/resurrection that is spoken of in the prophecy to Maccabees 7:v9, *'with his last breath he exclaimed,' cruel brute, you may discharge us from this present life but the king of the world will raise us up, since we die for his laws, to live again forever.'*

That InI know in the history of the bible,' the first reincarnation there was that of Shem, son of Noah, received the highest blessings and reincarnated 'Melchizedek', because of his work on the ark with the animals, he had reached the hola Mountain of the living supreme architect of heaven and earth.

Isaiah 11:v6-9, *'the wolf also shall dwell with the lamb, and the leopard shall lie down with the goat and the calf and the young lion and the yearling together. And a little child shall lead them, and the cow and the bear shall feed; their young ones shall lie down together; and the lion shall eat straw like the ox and the young child shall play on the hole of the cobra, and the young child shall put his hand into the vipers nest, they shall not hurt, nor destroy in all my holy Mountain; for the earth shall be full of the knowledge of the lord, as the waters cover the sea.'*

The new world, everything made new, gave Shem the title Melchizedek, interpretation 'king of righteousness, and also King of Sälem, which is king of peace, without father, without mother, without descent, having neither beginning of days, nor end of life, but made like unto the son of God, abideth a priest Itinually.

There in the new world, he 'Shem' was not physically born, he was a grown man at the start of that new world,(beginning) , knowing only the supreme architect as father of all creation, there were no personal claims there, Immortal he was made in his reincarnation he was given immortal life spirit from the ancient of days.

In the ark Shem was reincarnated Melchizedek the ark and the tabernacle are hola places, today the tabernacle its where Nyahbinghì is reincarnated, like wise in InI reincarnation, InI are reincarnated 'Nyahbinghì'.

Nyahbinghì has the same interpretation as Melchizedek, (same order) Nyahbinghì because of the reincarnation of the dead, to live with Christ in his kingly character imajesty Haile Selassie the 1st, and to forget never to remember the dead living ways of Babylon Rome sinful world, now because InI *the rapture* coming forward with Imajesty King Ras Tafari, InI receive that high blessings same as Melchezedek to remain of a priestly order forever.

Since Shem came from the old world and was saved, having to disassociate with the vain element of being a part of men and people of that past,' that had been destroyed, they (he) had to give up everything that was no more to be remembered, "the birth that he had back there"= giving him no beginning of days= Melchezedek order, giving him no ending of time, immortal= Ivine livity, for the most high supreme architect.

Shem had to forget any relation with that past world life, living or dead, in Shem Melchezedek soul heart Irits, he was not birth of Noah or Naamah Noah wife, Naamah had gave birth to triplets Shem, Ham and Ja-pheth.

Shem knowing that everything belongeth to the supreme architect, *'the only father of creation, the maker of heaven and earth is the only father and mother, no woman belongs to no man and no man belongs to no woman, all belongeth to the I AM that I AM.'*

Giving all glory and honour to The I AM that I AM, 'Shem Melchizedek having no beginning of days, because those days were destroyed (wiped out) an abomination gone and never to be remembered anymore, no ending of time, as death being a worldly concept from the material sense,' those thinking that body is self'.

As in Inl Nyahbinghì reincarnation and fire baptism, Babylon is never to be remembered anymore; Babylon world and ways are an abomination. Shem Melchezedek having ancestral linage would associated him with things and ways that were an abomination to the maker of heaven and earth, all were gone from him never to be remembered.

Shem was reincarnated Melchezedek in the ark, given Iternal life Ivine livity as Inl are reincarnated from *the rapture* in the tabernacle Nyahbinghì, Melchezedek is the same priestly order as Nyahbinghì. For a one to have entered into Ivine livity a one must be reincarnated of soul to attain Ivine Irits.

Inl with no beginning of days and no ending of time, to remain of a priestly order, Icracy tabernacle administration 'fire Ingel' forlver, not only that Shem was the blessings of the flood, he could of told what the 'I AM' (god) did and bear witness forlver. Whereas the Melchezedek intrusion explains that Abram himself was sustained by Melchezedek since he refused to consume of the luxury of Sodom because his Lord was of the non-material world.

The Torah explains that Melchezedek, essentially Shem, was given the priesthood, indeed Shem, he was 465 years old at the time they met and Abram was 75 years of age 'even Abraham was envious of Melchezedek' for asking him how he got off the ark. Melchizedek answered 'through merit and virtue merit (service).

Abram said but there was no other people there excepting your family, who did you have to show merit and virtue' Melchizedek said' we did not sleep day or night,' we had to feed the animals and care for them all through.

The Jewish Talmud book of Jewish Laws 1769 Seder ha-Dorot page nine, chazalic literature unanimously identify Melchezedek as Shem son of Noah and gives an account of priest Shem Melchezedek. Remember Inl (of king David throne) are the true seed of the Jew, Inl supreme authority is in Camp David ancient Dominion Empire the Rastafari house Ethiopia, Haile Selassie 1st is the 225 great grandson of Solomon and David.

Jeremiah chapter 8:v21, *'for the hurt of the daughter of my people am I hurt; I am black; Jeremiah says of himself' I am black',* he is a Jew in Jerusalem at the time of king Jo-sias King of Judah.

History tells that in earth Inl are the true Jews that came up from Egypt as Israel and became Jews because of the language Inl spoke' tribe of Judah also because of the region where Inl dwelleth, showed what tribe ones were of, Shem Melchizedek was a mystic to the people of the earth for who he was, because he had no beginning, where he came from was no more.

The supreme architect 'the I AM that I AM' also took the abominations away from them that they did not remember, only the transition of the ark where he gave them greater powers exulting them closer to him that those effects were extremely greater than the past, that their thoughts remained in the new and forgot the past world before the ark.

The separation that they made within their transition was a onetime thing that could not have been inherited by any one, who never made that journey, the same way that I Negus I Christ was not the same as his brothers and sisters, "Joseph children, as so for Shem being reincarnated unto Ivinity.

The same way that Nyahbinghì cannot be inherited at physical birth manifestation from father, or mother to child, only through reincarnation at fire baptism all new city's – Irits - and excellency decorations ,hola Ivictions are received, reincarnation is a transmigration of soul, brought to live in remembrance of the true ways of the world.

Inl ancient dominion empire in baptism of fire you are taken into Mount Zion gates camp David supreme authority and are given the title 'Nyahbinghì', it is not a name thing that you just pick up and start following, using the word loosely it is an administration of Inl supreme authority in earth.

Ingels pilgrimage Inl journey that is Nyahbinghì order, rather than on asserting one's personal rights, Inl tabernacle churchical administration order is an emergency first and forlver, it is eternal and *ivine,* giving self-up entirely to *the rapture* of Christ in his kingly character Nyahbinghì administration the ancient supremacy, renouncing worldly affairs similar to hermits or Batawi a hola livity sight up the vital need of carrying out disinterested thoughts and actions for the world of colonial values.

In first fulfilling *the rapture* 'most vital, not wanting to take part in the Roman Babylon world built on colonial values, colonial values, are great wealth, great possessions and power, the objects of worldly activity, the building of slave masteries sustainable society.

Inl are not of that world, an anglophile could never be Nyahbinghì, those are of this world, 'fire burn them, *the rapture* faith is complete Ifidence and trust in Christ majesty Haile Selassie 1st and Inl administration supremacy on account of Ivinity,' a strong truth knowledge not needing proof.

Just attending a Nyahbinghì Isis service administration gathering in ceremonial dressing where there is a fire burning, does not attribute to you a fire baptism, reincarnation is in the hands of the supreme architect ministered by the Ingels, those things does not happen outside a sacred prescribed tabernacle, Melchezedek is a title of the king priest of Sälem which is Irusalem.

Nyahbinghì is a title of the prince priest, prophet or fire Ingel of Zion heavenly Zion, a warrior of the new Irusalem" Ethiopia' (on earth), as when InI receive Nyahbinghì order sanctification from the world through reincarnation the reincarnation is from mortal Iration unto Ivine Iration, InI separation from the world, that world that has nothing prepared for those who do not accept the dogmatic, satanic, beast teachings handed down of the world for their expectations.

Ancestral linage beginning of days and time these things would hold InI to the world and the ways of the world, InI tradition is a cosmic tradition those worldly concepts are not to be remembered any more, they are all pollution and abomination, that is if ones are truly practicing living Nyahbinghì and not dealing in dualism.

In giving up the world and its ways, what ones see is Haile Selassie the 1st in the world, as a statesman 'that was his manifestation in Babylon as head of the Ethiopian world state.

My faith *the rapture* is not of this world,' the people of the world look upon Ras Tafari Makonnen they see Haile Selassie 1st, what they know of the world's teachings about him and his worldly activities as statesman, head of the Ethiopian Empire Emperor of Ethiopia yet, they fail to see further,' the meaning of "Haile Selassie," "power of the hola trinity."

The worldlians do not sight up that the power of the hola trinity could not be of the world; 'the power of the hola trinity is not a thing furnished by man, that cannot be constructed or applied through democracy or any worldly process it is not an organization.

Therefore, the worldlians miss the essential focus that identifies (tells who he is) Emperor Haile Selassie the 1st, all of the above shows that my faith the knowledge of InI faith is a secret to the world.

Imajesty Haile Selassie the 1st was and is the 'only one worthy' to do his works, loose the seven seals and represent InI in the world, as InI were captives in Babylon, Christ in his kingly character Imajesty had to come into Babylon to free InI, Iritcally, from under the authority of the colonial world sovereign throne.

Only the sovereign Christ in his kingly character could have broken the chains of the authority furnished in the world by the colonial throne, holding the people under its spells of sorceries. Christ in his kingly character came so that InI can trod out of Babylon world, not that InI should see know and hear them try to get personal powers and fame, "now that Babylon has fallen it cannot remain no more, when ones want to live in Babylon ways, many want to take Babylon Rome culture to Ethiopia/Africa, even more many don't know the live, many only know Roman-tick Babylon.

There is no comparison 'the king did that so you must do that', most of what ones saw of the king was in Babylon, the King is Mount Zion but went into Babylon to represent, InI are trod Mount Zion, trod up out of Babylon Rome and question not Haile Selassie the 1st, Haile Selassie the1st is Christ in his kingly character, there is only one Ras Tafari and that is Haile Selassie the 1st.

Haile Selassie the 1st owns the earth and he is the I AM that I AM in the physical of man Nyahbinghi is not god, Aba Janhoy is the almighty InI Nyahbinghi *the rapture* are the Ingels, InI faith is administered Icracy (churchically).

Those who take the order must trod up forward and leave worldly matters, the order is the faith InI are not worldly, it is not the material body of the attendants its InI soul spirit, Irits essence cosmic principles that is the church, InI are to administer only in Icracy and "work in Rastafari Itrades for comforts and protection, shelter, cloths and food (material & money) means being one with the cosmic, to make InI self-most enjoyable in this live.

Healers, priests of all soul spirits supreme to all beings more cosmology than earthly, though tending to mother earth, carers of soil and all living thing that needs protection from the biological pest known as leper; preserve the earth and its produce, for from the spirit of the earth InI shall get a feed forward, care for the animals, love all little children, (see psalms 137:v9) whether they are biological Japhethians, black, red or yellow. Nyahbinghi's commitments are Mount Zion heaven; Ingels are only here in rapture with Christ in his kingly character Haile Selassie 1st and Empress Menen to do I works, not to have social commitments with the world at present now.

InI Iternal kingempire is Zion in cosmology heaven, until Christ in his kingly character Haile Selassie the 1st thy kingdom come on earth as it is in heaven Ethiopia earthly kingdom. 'To turn aside from everything that leads astray 'is to turn aside from the world, attachment can be a great barrier to spiritual livity. Attachment to anything that is not Iternal is a burden, i.e. "cares of the world", Iternal life does not include the pride of vanities visible earth bound material, away from Ivinity the body flesh is dominated by the world, the more money/material that ones have the less ones shall know I fullness Nyahbinghi Rastafari way of life.

Nyahbinghi I chant 'Babylon take your bag of money and go', "do not take money for my way of life", It appears that many Nyahbinghi brethren are chasing after governments of the world and governments of the island for training for Ras'es into professionalism and ways of the world. This is not the trod of those who have achieved renunciation from the world, to attain offices in the institutions of the world of Camp David, in the USA that holds their seal.

(Armageddon is the complete destruction of Babylon world) - burn Rome -, that is not Nyahbinghi tradition it's not *the rapture*, they do not know *the rapture* Rastafari is I life, theocracy Ivine livity spiritual observance life first. Ones cannot reach I fullness through blessings of material abundance whereas spiritual blessings, yes, Nyahbinghi is a spiritual journey passing through earth.

St John 14:v17-19, ' *the spirit of truth, the world cannot accept him, because it neither sees him nor knows him, but you know him, for he lives with you and will be in you, I will not leave you comfortless, I will come to you.* '

A Saint of the Ethiopian orthodox church, 'InI brethren' "St Gebre Kristos,' this Ethiopian prince sacrificed all his belongings to lead a life of chastity and ended up a leprous beggar, he's usually depicted outside his palace, where only his dogs now recognize him'.

A capitalist cannot enter the hola Mountain, a capitalist cannot trod Mount Zion I, those that trade in products that they do not produce themselves, or that the product is not of Rastafari livity foundation, relating to InI nation hood(Africa).

If Ras'es are not the foundation producers, then they are taking part in a worldly organization, pushing goods for the oppressors, upholding Babylon world and colonial values, working for the world for gains and rewards. They are worldly and have not control of their means, they are an agent for Babylon, those are not Nyahbinghi they are not I rapture; they are maintaining what should be falling and trampled underfoot.

Upon I hola Mountain Mount Zion, it is not for the love of creatures that creatures are dear, but for the love of the soul in animals that animals are dear, 'I AM' that I AM supreme architect (God) showed that in Shem Melchezedek and the ark.

The conquering lion Haile Selassie 1st of I hola Mountain, whereas the (organization of Africa unity) all have the power of animal magnetism, element of object in mind object of sense of the beasts of the earth, animal object Africa land until African states and nationals can live man, woman and child in unity, true love, or compassion.

The ministry of reconciliation that I Negus I Christ prepared (for Congo supremacy) Mount Zion I hola Mountain, where there is no blood sacrifice,' beef will not be the favourite dish', all flesh mouth must go so that their Irits could perceive the cosmic Iration. Mount Zion the Hola Mountain carries an Ital Irits.

Haile Selassie the 1st art the I Negus I Christ who trod the earth over two thousand years ago the Messiah, The Saviour, Mädhane, the first born son of the dead, the light of the world, "the way of live", he and the father being one, having the hola Irits all in one. I Negus I Christ (iyäsus) Imajesty took no part in worldly affairs in his first advent.

Yet constantly did the work of the 'I AM' raised the dead in flesh and spirit, heals the sick, gave sight to the blind material and spiritual, preformed all sorts of miracles. At that time administered a theocractical order only, separated from the world, not of the world, that is the way InI are to follow Christ in his kingly character, living Icracy reign having no leader other than Haile Selassie the 1st.

That's the only way ones will know Mount Zion as a hola place, recognizing no leader, only Haile Selassie the 1st Imajesty and recognizing InI Nyahbinghi Ingels

the rapture coming through earth in this time with Christ in his kingly char/
Second Advent walking in the administration of Nyahbinghi tabernacle.

The Rapture a priestly order, from InI ancient Dominion Empire InI are not of the
world InI are of *the rapture* Haile Selassie the1st manifested, went in to Babylon
world to deal with stately matters as a statesman he was the chosen one the only
worthy one.

The same Haile Selassie the 1st did not preach, practice InI faith in his world
representation of the black nation; head of O.A.U (organisation African unity); head
of the Ethiopian Orthodox Church; the branch of Jesse on King David throne. Christ
in his kingly character 'for all is his', Nyahbinghi is not God and Nyahbinghi *the
rapture* are not statesman for the world or of the world.

InI are Ethiopians (Africans) warriors in earth, Ingels of Mount Zion that is InI Iternal
home not earth, our Iternal place is InI home InI are only passing through for needs
to fulfil the prophecies, establish the Iternal sovereign. Earth is a material kingdom,
our material home, where material reign, that is why Haile Selassie the 1st decent
had to be published and known: HIM had to have the highest honour in material
sense, and yet be the supreme architect spiritual being in material quality (Solomon,
I Negus I Christ rises from king David).

Many that claim the title Nyahbinghi do not know their portfolio or the administration,
InI are not statesman InI are fire Ingels following Christ in his kingly character,
priestly Icracy order living the ancient Dominion Empire Supreme authority in this
modern time. Those whose minds are possessed on earthly things, livity because
they have not the spirit, their destiny is destruction, to perish with a world of illusions
that has already ended.

Chapter Six

Iritical Ivictions

Inl Nyahbinghi known as *the rapture* Iritical Ivictions…

The devil Lucifer that old dragon, Revelation 12:v9, *'and the great dragon was cast out, that old serpent, called the devil and Satan, which deceiveth the whole world, he was cast out into the earth, and his angels were cast out with him, and all the nations were beasts in the devils world, the most powerful administration that ruled the world is the devils administration.'*

The dragon (America) and includes the rest of the world that gave power to the beast, Revelation 13:v4 *'and they worshipped the dragon which gave power unto the beast, and they worshiped the beast, saying who is like unto the beast? Who is able to make war unto him? The beast that had risen out of the sea.'*

Revelation 13:v1-3 *'and I stood upon the sand of the sea, and I saw a beast rise up out of the sea, having seven heads and ten horns, and upon his horns ten crowns, and upon his heads the name of blasphemy, 'and the beast which I saw was like unto a leopard, and his feet were as the feet of a bear and his mouth as the mouth of a lion, and the dragon gave him his power, and his seat, and great authority, and i saw one of his heads as it were wounded to death and his deadly wound was healed, and all the world wondered after the beast.'*

The beast's seven heads was the old Roman Empire and the ten crowns are those countries that were colonies of the Roman Empires. The beast's leopard form represents Germany its feet represents Russia and the mouth Spain the European Caucasian nations that carried it.

The one head of the beast that was wounded represented the Roman church, the wound was when the old Roman Empire split, dismantled, and the Roman Church was not actively instated in the new world power internationally.

The wound was healed when the Pope Paul VI first returned into America 2nd July 1963 met with the President John. F Kennedy, the Pope Paul VI kissed the ground and got reinstated office in the world church of the world power America.

That old dragon the devil Lucifer, the leader of the world, prepares a world for his son the anti-Christ. He builds a shrine for the anti-Christ in his land, 'Hollywood movie world, the devils angels 'movie stars' administer there, their immortality is a material preservation of their material image in the screen vision, they are the nation of that land America and envision it out into the world for the multitudes to worship them and give praises through the medium TV and screen goddess worship.

The anti-Christ established the shrine then went into the white house 'William Peter Blanty' in his book 'the exorcist' revealed Ronald Reagan to be the anti- Christ. Ronald Reagan's daughter Pattie Reagan was a main architect and administrator of Hollywood movie world, the American anti-Christ administration, from Hollywood to the White House (Ronnie anti-Christ Reagan) he the anti-Christ being the one that came from the anti-Christ life shrine movie world, he Reagan received the highest decorations and glory of Hollywood that there will ever be in their world to get the American world white house god seat and to rule the world.

The old dragon Lucifer makes himself visible to the world in the personality of Ronald Reagan as the father and the son are one, demonstrating the anti-Christ seat of power in the world that is the American administration. The beast and the dragon are one church and state of the colonial Roman world, carrying their sovereign crown, Revelation 17:v5, 'and upon her forehead was a name written, mystery Babylon the great, the mother of harlots and abominations of the earth.' They worship the beast that carries the whore of Babylon Buckinhamdeath.

Revelation 17:v3, 'so he carried me away in the spirit into the wilderness, and I saw a woman sit upon a scarlet coloured beast, full of names of blasphemy, having seven heads and ten horns.'

Revelation 13:v18, 'here is wisdom, let him that hath understanding count the number of the beast, for it is the number of a man, and his number is six hundred threescore and six,' 666 the number on the mightier (hat) worn by the pope of Rome 'the one who stands in the place of the Christ to the world.

The worldlians follow the dragon (American world order) and the beast Rome world church, the beast carries the woman whore house administration all through the earth; as there is only one queen for the Roman Jesus churches in the world, churches affiliated to gentile Jesus does not go without the queen of Babylon Rome Buckingham.

Revelation 17:v4, 'and the woman was arrayed in purple and scarlet colour, and decked with gold and precious stones and pearls, having a golden cup in her hand full of abominations and filthiness of her fornications.'

When other nations build shrines dedicated in the movie world, Bollywood, Nollywood etc., these are same shrines for worship unto the anti-Christ because the movie world is the anti-Christ world. The dragon anti-Christ, beast and the great mother of harlots are one in agreement.

Babylon world church and state's these are what forms the spirit of the world, this is what the spirit worldlians are made of, the world and those of the world can never love ones after ones have trodden forward and left out of the world as ones have rebuked all that they are.

So don't be as those that try to go back into Babylon world through music and joining other organizations that cooperate together in Roman Babylon world, just dry up your tears and come up. The spirit of the world dies when ones face the fire baptism of Nyahbinghi reincarnation the rapture.

Ones claiming to be in Ivinity must Isider and able to reveal how they arrived in InI Ivine Iternal Iivity, for it takes a reincarnation to arrive in Ivinity, that is a ceremonial Iritical decorations handed down, furnished unto a one administered by higher exulted fire Ingels high priests. It is impossible for anyone to come to Ivinity on their own outside of a Nyahbinghì tabernacle.

I man sight that in the future Europe and America shall offer and set a crown upon the head that they shall call sacred, a king that they will choose and allowed to be appointed in the land that they have called this modern day democracy Israel, when that king is crowned there, he will become the patriarch of the world, then they will continue to counterfeit him for the Christ of David's throne as they publish him as the patriarch of the world.

InI way of live is in the Nyahbinghì chants, ones must listen to the Binghì songs 'the administration way of live, Mount Zion through Congo supremacy. Christ in his kingly character Haile Selassie the 1st manifestation in Babylon to deal with stately matters, everything the King Ras Tafari did is perfectly correct. He represented InI in the world and showed InI his great kingdom outside of the world, camp David ancient dominion empire there he represents InI also as everywhere.

The whole of I heart is Nyahbinghì and I Irits heavens are *the rapture* tabernacle administration of cosmic principle on account of throne dominion and powers.
In the days of visitation hearts are open and some hearts beat for the world power wanting material rewards.

Fame is a material reward because its value is in the world, all Nyahbinghì sins are forgiven in *the rapture* gathering, Romans 8:v1-2 *'therefore there is now no condemnation for those who are in I Negus I Christ Imajesty because through Christ Imajesty the law of the spirit of life set I free from the law of sin and death.'*

I have made many references to the New Testament because that is where InI are most *the rapture* of Christ in his kingly character with InI the Ingels in the times of the modern world.

The Hola Herb 'Ishence'

Inl hola sacrament Idicated to King Solomon, the hola herb is Inl hola sacrament Inl special grace presentation Inl use the sacred herb to serve Christ in his kingly character Haile Selassie 1st. To search in Inl irits-heavens (consciousness) to see the ancient way, how to see Inl life and the ways of fellowship to find out what is true and correct to see truths and love.

Inl hola herb Ishence that was first found growing on King Solomon grave. Was said to of have Itained the wise mind of King Solomon, "herb of the Wiseman" that hola sacrament herb has from that time been Idicated to King Solomon. Idication to King Solomon makes Inl hola sacrament herb becomes 'sacred' Inl special grace offering, "sacred is hola." That hola herb Inl use in communication with the supreme architect,' that increases Inl knowledge in Icentration Iditation Irits perceivement that introverts inner Iritual, spiritual (Icepts), wiseman, spiritual inner self knowledge 'reward is absent.

Inl hola sacrament herb is used in hola service worship, giving isis and thanks offerings to Christ in his kingly character Haile Selassie 1st and become visible reality mix with the unseen. Inl hola sacramental herb is the freeman key, keyman to new overstandings in commune with Inl spiritual soul self that travels the whole galaxies now passing earth.

Inl hola sacrament strengthens Inl in Inl cosmic tradition. Beelzebub Lucifer's worlds are afraid of Inl hola herb, the dragon the beast with the harlot and the anti-Christ has outlawed Inl hola sacrament herb in their world. Because Inl hola herb is a 'man' Solomon, "King Solomon" when diagnosed it makes live the Solomanic destiny Iration, 'the original ways of the world Inl supreme authority that is Inl destiny, nationhood, culture, true identity, that is Inl spirituality Solomonical same Davidical throne one Ras Tafarical destiny, Christ in his kingly character from Shem Melchezedek. Inl destiny to the Ras Tafari house on earth Zion Ethiopia Camp David ancient dominion empire Haile Selassie 1st throne land Africa.

The Love Of Nyahbinghì Children

Collectively as a nation InI are the nation of King Ras Tafari the children of King Ras Tafari Haile Selassie the 1st being the nation of Shem Melchizedek.

InI *the rapture* reincarnated Nyahbinghì, InI perfect love and the love of the world is not the same that is also how InI are not of the world, Nyahbinghì are children of those of InI that have children. InI are ones and one's children in InI sacred Rastafari family love.

Ones is sited as children as ones comes into InI faith Nyahbinghì in love, surely on account of the reincarnation InI are children walking now in ivinity whether grown up or young, children of a knowledgeable one already in Nyahbinghì faith Rastafari family livity, that is Nyahbinghì children Rastafari livity, in life love and cosmic Iternal, being children of a brethren/sistren children that a one has, a one must have that Iple that the brethren/sistren is blessing a one becoming, even being called by that child name 'the highest acknowledgement of Nyahbinghì family love, Nyahbinghì children in InI sacred family love.

One could be a child of a one who does not have children to represent that one, only the youth being grown will manifest only the elder as well as others that the elder has grown are brethren and sistren, it is always strength to strength although it is always greater love and strength when the elder has children in Rastafari to give and receive strength.

That way is the ultimate strength in InI truths, InI are always in a strength, followers follow until they receive fire baptism and are reincarnated into Ivinity where the hola Irits dwell, in Nyahbinghì fire baptism they are become children of InI children. Followers are recognised through attendance, yet they are not reincarnated souls through the fire baptism.

That is InI Nyahbinghì love everything according to InI administration and not the present Babylon world. The love that there is in InI Rastafari family Nyahbinghì in perfect love is the highest of strength, a Ivine love it is a sacred hola Rastafari family love.

Christ in his kingly character Haile Selassie 1st is mediator, judge, actor and orator above all in InI administration in my way of life, in my livity InI are ones and one's children, ones just don't come in to InI way of life just so, there is no self-appointed spokesman, InI are in Nyahbinghì livity being children of an elder in knowledge of InI administration.

Any that appears in InI way of live without having InI faith's administrative elder brethren/mama in this present time is such a wolf! Who grow you? Must be television screen vision the music industry, institutions, universities and colleges which are the anti-Christ teachers, teaching organs supporting the ways of the world.

The elder Kingman/Empress are not looking any world substance of a one growing in InI faith, all that InI are administering that one's love Nyahbinghì with all ones whole heart in *the rapture* cosmic Irits, Nyahbinghì children.

I AM THAT I AM, Exodus 3:v14-15, *'and god said unto Moses, I AM THAT I AM; and he said, thus shalt thou say unto the children of Israel (Jacob) , 'I AM' hath sent me unto you, and the I AM said moreover unto Moses, thus shalt thou say unto the children of Israeli "Jacob" the lord god of your fathers, the god of Abraham, the god of Isaac, and the god of Jacob, hath sent me unto you; this is my name 'forever,' and this is my memorial unto all generations.'*

InI Nyahbinghì *the rapture* forIver use the word "I AM" in calling the I AM RAS TAFARI supreme architect name, Christ in his kingly character Haile Selassie the 1st, Nyahbinghì I rapture InI.

Before King James version of the bible and the Anglo Saxon (English) church (same Roman church) which said "translated out of the original tongues and with the former translations diligently compared and revised, the name Jah or Jahovah, was not a name known for InI supreme architect.

The I AM therefore InI *the rapture* Nyahbinghì use I AM (ellohim) InI interpret the word god and call 'I AM' in his true name the " I AM" and that is InI supreme architect Imajesty name forIver, Haile Selassie the 1st the 'I AM' RAS TAFARI.

Now when a man is speaking he cannot be breathing and talking at the same time, this is the order of the cosmic, of breath to speech and when a man is breathing he cannot be speaking, in that same said way when you are dealing with worldly matters you cannot be living Nyahbinghì, at that time you are not living in Ivine livity.

InI are fire Ingels *the rapture* Nyahbinghì warriors reincarnated in the fire baptism. Brethren that have not been reincarnated InI fire baptism and from the ungodly teachings of the world, as well as the desires of their natures.

It is because of fear (lack of knowledge) and lack of adoration for Ras Tafari emperor Haile Selassie the 1st, king of kings' lord of lords conquering lion of Judah. They have to acknowledge *the rapture* for recognition of InI faith, in recognition by the world, the heavenly throne of Ras Tafari Makonnen, *the black Christ* recognised and chosen head of the Nyahbinghì known to the world as *the rapture*.

Ones must sight up the Irits of the administration to recognise the authority the administration functions from the tabernacle altar, InI faith' through the administering Ingels, prince, prophet, priests. It is all about 'the fire baptism reincarnation', the decorations that a one receives during that time and furnishings through greater knowledgeable ones.

Those ones that came into the Nyahbinghì faith Rastafari life, not entering through the tabernacle, are in Rome, being not reincarnated; they carry a world spirit belonging to the beast and the anti-Christ which is the whore house administration.

Those have not been reincarnated, they live in Balaam's house of reggae/dance that they have built in Israel which isn't black love (divine love) neither solidarity 'there is no reincarnation to Ivine livity in reggae musical entertainment; there they have world authority to the level that the world allows them.

Those ways isn't Nyahbinghi' according to their works for the world and their institutional decorations or ways taught to them by the world. They have blessings from worldly organizations, music corporations, industries and all the things that they support, that they give their most to, as the race horse gambling shops, the great tobacco and cigarette barons, the stout dragon and rum barons.

Their blessings are handed down to them from world powers, down the line to them from companies, firms, agencies and the systematic role, they are qualified shitsteamatic solders of Babylon, they have authority from the beast and the dragon.

They have no authority in or from Nyahbinghi administration, they have no authority from a place called Zion in Ethiopia Camp David Ancient Dominion Empire, authority in Nyahbinghi is Ivine 'only' because ones couldn't have it without reincarnation and it's only given through Ivine love that the world does not know.

From Israel the man' son of Isaac came the Israelites, until David established Irusalem those that dwelt there (all Judah some Benjamines also the Levites) because the Ark of the Covenant was with the king of Judah (David). All became known as Jews via the language they spoke also of the region that they dwelled in.

Solomon the Jew, son of David, I Negus I Christ (born) manifest in flesh in Bethlehem a Jew sematic. Ras Tafari the same Christ in his kingly character from Solomon the Jew royal seed; Menlik the 1st Solomon son with the queen of Sheba; Makkedah in Ethiopia Ras Tafari the Christ in his kingly character royal true Jew seed of Solomon through Menlik the 1st. Haile Selassie the 1st the return Christ in his kingly character to reign through David flesh and blood.

Inl faith is not Rastafari, Rastafari is Inl way of life (way of live) Inl faith is Nyahbinghi which is *the rapture*, Imajesty return 'the rescue, the second appearance of the messiah Christ in his kingly character with Inl', keeping his promise he had made to the apostles.

St John 14:v3, *'and if I go and prepare a place for you, I will come again, and receive you unto myself that where I am there ye may be also, known as the rapture, a place prepared,'* now returned to show Inl the way to live on earth, through Inl faith in *the rapture* of Christ in his kingly character, in divinity (Ivine livity) until restoration unto Iternal life forIver.

As for those who are waiting for the I Negus I Christ to return, there is no place prepared for them as he said he shall return once that place has been prepared. Rastafari faith is the return of the messiah Christ in his kingly character, Inl glory is that king Ras Tafari has kept his promise to Inl that know him.

The churches of the world seem to think that after I Negus I Christ rose, was risen after three days, that was his return thus then have spiritualised David's throne forIver, 'saying it's not a throne in earth it's in heaven but at that time he had not gone away as yet, he had not ascended at that time, as he had made that clear to those who saw him then, "he had not yet ascended to the father.

The followers of Rome (democracy) unorthodox Christians are saying that Christ is spirit 'that Christ has no colour, meaning that Christ has no flesh, must read, 'the 2nd Epistle of John, v 7, *'for many deceivers are entered in to the world, who confess not that iyäsus Christ is not come in the flesh, this is a deceiver and an anti-Christ.'*

Although the dying thief on the cross was with him (I Negus I Christ) in paradise on that day, he could not have prepared his full glory in those three days.

Rastafari faith is in *the rapture*, and that is Christ in his kingly character in his second advent, the world will have to catch up with InI *the rapture* and recognise Haile Selassie the 1st as the Christ in his kingly character and drop their fears and live for a righteous government Icracy reign not political, because there is no rapture without Christ in his kingly character returning in the flesh and blood with ten thousands of his saints and Ingels. The world and their false teachings of I Negus I Christ is spirit only and the so-called true Christian worship is rebuked by InI and Christ in his kingly character, for InI faith carries commands and 'rebukes.

Rebuke because they are denying the temple (body) of I Negus I Christ and his throne, saying 'Christ is a spirit and king David's throne is in heaven, spiritualising the throne and saying Christ has no body (they are not identifying him in flesh) although they make a big fuss about his blood, ask yourself 'is there blood that doesn't come from a body, the blood of Christ must have flesh as a temple for the spirit to dwell, to sit upon David's throne, InI all know that David's throne is realistic on earth as Caesar's throne is in Rome.

Chapter Seven

Recognition

In the modern world today, for recognition of InI true loving Ivine faith 'Nyahbinghi, the world will have to see and know InI through the eyecept of *the rapture*. In the twinkle of an eye one will sight InI cosmic tradition that is the complete *rapture* of the messiah return of Christ in his kingly character with InI to show InI his glory and gathering of InI selves unto him. Imajesty Ras Tafari Haile Selassie the 1st, Nyahbinghi faith is *the rapture*.

The rapture come forward through Haile Selassie the 1st, InI faith is in Haile Selassie the 1st, for was it not for Haile Selassie 1st, InI Nyahbinghi *the rapture* could not have come forward, that I faith would grow and live.

The world should overstand, comprehend Nyahbinghi faith for mankind to know it is called *the rapture*, of the nominations, Ethiopian orthodox, 12 tribes, Bobo Ashanty, InI Nyahbinghi, InI are *the rapture* the orthodox faith sprang (rooted) from the first advent before the new name of the messiah and his return in the personality of Ras Tafari Haile Selassie the 1st, the Christ in his kingly character has said that InI are Orthodox unto the end of the world.

In 1930 recognised black Christ head of the Nyahbinghi/ *rapture*; ones will clearly see that the love and the faith are a black love and a black faith. That Nyahbinghi stands for black supremacy, the colour of Ivine (divine) is black, therefore black love means Ivine love, again a black faith means a Ivine faith the supremacy means that immortal is supreme to mortal, so black supremacy means Ivine supremacy.

InI tradition a Ivine livity, where does it stand for those who are trying to live the way of the world "statesmen" and InI sanctification (separation) from the world of the dragon, the beast, the anti-Christ and the whore of Babylon, again I say to you that people of the world do not have Nyahbinghi faith. The balance is that InI faith is a million miles away from evil.

Only in Ivine theocracy and through *the rapture* InI in 'the prepared place' shall true redemption prevail from the world and democracy. In the modern world InI shall be known as *the rapture*, the tabernacle administration of Nyahbinghi the Ingels in *the rapture* of Christ in his kingly character.

Haile Selassie the 1st the Second Advent, theocracy order, tabernacle churchical administration, Nyahbinghi order, in recognition in the modern world 'the 1st so called world.' Nyahbinghi has been known in the third world, Africa the Caribbean but not in the so called 1st world.

In the modern world, when people hear that word 'Nyahbinghi' they think it's purely tribal, "well in truth it is an African tribe thing", the Nyahbinghi *the rapture* are families of African tribes dwelling in the Caribbean and Africa and places of the earth today but it will not be asserted, accepted in the modern world as a faith because Nyahbinghi isn't biblical scriptural.

The rapture is scriptural, the tribes of it is the chain InI link InI connection as one as a nation of same, the ones that are *the rapture* the heavenly Issembly, are the ones that came with Christ in his kingly character the returned messiah is the head of it.

In 1935 newspapers of the world told that Haile Selassie the 1st is the head of the mighty cult of warriors of Nyahbinghì in Africa, in earth Nyahbinghì = an African tribe thing, 1930 in a secret meeting of 82 African delegates, his imperial Imajesty Haile Selassie the 1st was crowned chosen king leader of the Nyahbinghì. In Moscow also states leaders in Africa elected him head the black Christ according to prophecy and Revelation reveals to Rastafari denomination that Haile Selassie the 1st of Ethiopia is the Christ in his kingly character returned.

After more than two thousand years in *the rapture*, that is in InI faith 'that is Nyahbinghì at its highest point and there is Nyahbinghì in Africa not knowing that they are the heavenly (Issembly) on earth, feet and body of that head creator Imajesty Haile Selassie the 1st.

They are warriors fighting for material, personal power, doing other men's will, thinking that there are other leaders, when there is only one leader Christ in his kingly Haile Selassie the 1st" and no other, Nyahbinghì is biblical it's the order of Melchezedek which is a Iternal livity.

It is an Ivine livity that means there is an reincarnation unto Ivinity, that is where the Ingels in rapture reincarnate into Nyahbinghì, *the rapture* is biblical, people of the world' think that Nyahbinghì faith is not spoken of in the bible, but they will only recognise Nyahbinghì faith and know Nyahbinghì, in the name that is in the modern world, *the rapture*, known to the Ible, then ones shall know that Haile Selassie the 1st is Christ in his kingly character the messiah, recognition of InI faith is to know it as *the rapture*, 'they shall tell you in the modern world of InI *the rapture*.'

Those in the modern world will not overstand Nyahbinghì. 'Nyahbinghì' will be interpreted for their overstanding *the rapture*, in the modern world InI will be called *the rapture*.

For historians will teach of Nyahbinghì as an African movement warriors which fought against colonial occupiers of the 19th century up to the 1950's, relating to a earlier queen of Rwanda whose name was Queen Nyahbinghì or had a similar name Nyavinghi; as a tribe that rose in the name of a warrior spiritual priestess queen of Rwanda, 'she that possesses many things.'

In truths she is and they are Nyahbinghì warriors, but *the rapture* are those who come with Haile Selassie the 1st, declaring the tabernacle Icracy faith through the messiah Christ in his second advent return in his kingly character, with InI fire Ingels warriors, at the higher top of the administration Mount Zion, identifying Christ in his kingly character Ras Tafari further more identifying the anti-Christ the beast and the whore of Babylon in their personalities, balanced scale theocracy tabernacle Issembly administration (tabernacle).

The reason why InI portion of the Nyahbinghì is known as *the rapture* "because of the coming forward with the Christ in his kingly character it's the jewel of the

Nyahbinghì Inl being in Ivinity = Revelation 4:v4 and Revelation 5:v11, hence queen Nyahbinghì also the 82 African delegates they all have relations with Haile Selassie the 1st yet none of those Nyahbinghì claimed to be the Ingels and saints coming from the place where I Negus I Christ ascended to (heavenly Mount Zion) and returned from 'hence' Ethiopia.

Known as *the rapture* Christ in his kingly character with Inl, *the rapture* are those of the Nyahbinghì that are the reincarnation into Ivine live that have the reference to 'of being in heavens heavenly Issembly with Haile Selassie the 1st the conquering lion of the tribe of Judah, Christ in his kingly character of the scriptures through King David and Solomon of Irusalem Christ of Irusalem Haile Selassie the 1st.

In the new Irusalem Ethiopia is the indwelling place of the 'I AM' supreme architect Ras Tafari, where the Ark of the Covenant dwells and the only rainbow circle ensigned throne room on earth. Give thanks to Inl Iternal King Haile Selassie the 1st, 'for the glory that he has given to Inl.'

The elect of the heavenly Issembly that came forward with Christ in his kingly character and know Nyahbinghì through Haile Selassie the 1st, is the way that Imajesty has prepared for Inl as Africans. To be warriors, fire Ingels, of a priestly order for the King Christ throne of Ethiopia, that is he whom is spoken of in all the earth as son and father and hola one all in one.

Rapture Nyahbinghì has come from cosmic heaven and Nyahbinghì who was and is on earth, the head glory of the tabernacle Icracy administration, comes to identify with the whole body of the foundation the claim of *the rapture* being Ingels and saints with Christ in his kingly character.

Nyahbinghì warriors in earth who knew not they were belonging to the priestly order of the living "I AM" THAT I AM' through all ages, the one same family the head of power knowledge, glory, honour, praises and strength and the body of power and strength, that has its honour and glory through the head creator Haile Selassie the 1st and all who are glorified in Haile Selassie the 1st; becomes one in reincarnation.

Imajesty Christ Adonai Ras Tafari the 'I AM' forever guides and keep Inl enraptured soul (reincarnated souls), how can Inl be Ingels, if not for the resurrection, the living are those living in I Negus I Christ, living in the great 'I AM that I AM' the reincarnated from the dead are those whose messiah Christ in his kingly character has returned, after going away and preparing a place for them.

Those who are awaiting for the messiah I Negus I Christ to return, has no palace prepared for them, they are the dead in Christ and they live only because of the world, from a material sense, their glory is in this world, now the living in Imajesty Christ Ras Tafari Haile Selassie the 1st see Mark 12:v26 to 27, *'now about the dead rising- have you not read in the book of Moses, in the account of the bush, how god said to him, 'I am the god of Abraham, the god of Isaac, and the god of Jacob? He is not the god of the dead, but of the living you are badly mistaken.'*

Well when the 'I AM is telling Congo Moses these things, those whom he speaks of were all already dead in flesh, although they are living spirit (soul) what really counts, 'they are not dead, that why he said he is their god, and they can never die, the flesh is not the life Iternal, use your third eye for only the third I enters beyond the seven seals.

Knowing that Nyahbinghì is *the rapture* ones will overstand ones self more clear, in the Caribbean Nyahbinghì teachings varies from island to island, 'where there is more love, there is more fullness of truths and closer to the heart of the cities of Rastafari way of life, according to the love that is amongst the tabernacle and the knowledge the teachings of the administrating Ingels are there in love and skill power, some Binghì ones can join organizations become EWF(Ethiopian world Federation) members, become of the world, some can live a reggae life = leave Mount Zion *i*rits and dwell in Israel.

When a one is in reggae house, they are not in Ivinity, they are not trodding Mount Zion, in their reggae dance they are praising Diana of Ephesus, daughter of Zusus, see acts of the Apostles chapter 19:v27 *'so that not only this our craft is in danger to be set at nought, but also that the temple of the great goddess Diana should be despised and her magnificence should be destroyed, whom all Asia and the world worshipped... '* (read the whole of chapter 19)

There are those that say they are the ancient prophets that have returned, Elijah, Isaiah etc. but InI are *the rapture* the Ingels *that* is InI faith knowledge in remembrance Nyahbinghì that is in InI teachings.

Chapter Eight

In The Twinkling Of An Eye

Recognition means the renewing of one's mind from mortal material senses, to spiritual Ivine senses, essence Iternal (Ivine Livity). Material senses carry world powers, Ivine spiritual senses carries cosmic powers. In worshiping Christ in his kingly character High Majesty, Haile Selassie the1st, king Ras Tafari.

The service of InI Ingels Nyahbinghi, the sacrifice of being a worshiper is to discard and repudiate the world of Babylon today. The time of the first advent of I Negus I the Christ they came to renew their minds, following to change putting down the love of attachments to material sense and receiving the reaches of Ivine Iritual living.

Luke 14 v 26, 'If anyone comes to me and does not hate his father and mother, his wife and children, his brothers and sisters, 'yes even his own life, he cannot be my disciple.' Therefore they have no love for the world the ways of the world and concepts teachings of the worldly life etc., the apostle Paul speaks of it in Ephesians 4:v23, 'To be made new in the attitude of your mind.'

The renewing of one's mind is the reincarnated soul that wakes the dead mind of the world renewed to live, for I Negus I Christ in his kingly character Haile Selassie 1st and to forever be in I Negus I Christ king Ras Tafari. There are several references to renewing of one's mind in the Ible in II Corinthians 4v16, 'the soul gives life to the mind and the mind operates the sense organs.'

Recognition comes through receiving truths and knowledge of InI true identity in faith through that knowledge ones free will heart of love knowing its livity shall secure redemption from the world.

The objects themselves from material senses gives perceptions to mind and body when ones attention (desires) are stronger for all that is outside of the inner I (self) that one is away from InI administration, the whole of InI heart is Nyahbinghi and InI soul is cosmic heavens(Irits) of the rapture, for InI administration is an inbound Icept.

Renewing the mind (the Irits) through reincarnation a transition from mortal worldly material senses, forwarded to Ivine Immortal Iritual living senses.

There are those that have given up their soul from being their first love, in place to love the world, their vanities and the ways and things of the world. Whether by choice or constrained to do another man's will on their last judgment day they must get paid, St John chapter 16:v12-15, 'I have much more to say to you more than you can now bear, but when He, the spirit of truth comes, He will guide you into all truths, He will not speak on His own, He will speak only what he hears, and he will tell you what is yet to come, He will bring glory to me by taking from what is mine and making it known to you. All that belongs to the Father is mine. That is why I said the spirit will take from what is mine and make it known to you.'

Give thanks for the Irits of Nyahbinghi *the rapture* are essences cosmic principles

For recognition of the faith of the Second Advent of Christ in his kingly character Haile Selassie the 1st, InI faith-knowledge of InI true identity, knowledge of *the Rapture* (InI Nyahbinghi cosmic tradition.

Now the loosing of the seven seals that InI six senses can overpower the world and the ways of the world now that InI know the way prepared by Christ in his kingly character Haile Selassie the 1st. Through the Nyahbinghi administration InI can reach the inner kingman (kingdom) of the ancient dominion empire that had brought forward the outer universes of the galaxy, from the inner I.

InI now know the inner chamber of the Nyahbinghi administration where dwells the thrones of the house of King David and the supreme architect creation master of all in one King Ras Tafari. InI the 24 elders and all Nyahbinghi Ingels and saints InI Supreme Architect is always with InI and InI are never alone in Rastafari way of life. Haile Selassie the 1st ancient Ethiopian way of life Nyahbinghi faith, *the rapture* cosmic tradition.

The "I" means the Ivine soul Irits not the spirit of the world that the worldly work their minds from, the inner I the living I soul Irits are essence cosmic principles.
The I that lives forIver is invisible and also "Ivine visible" the worldly takes what they can see to be themselves. What they call me or you – these six sense organs are eyes, ears, nose, tongue, body and mind, the six senses are objects from sound, smell, taste, tactile objects and objects of mind.

The workings of the six sense consciousness, eye consciousness, ear consciousness and mind consciousness, these material based functions for sense perception arises because of contact between a sense organ and a sense object.

One must acknowledge that the material sense has not been the Ivine living I, (the self) that is Iternal. To transcend the concepts of the world teachings of death, to know there is neither beginning nor end to the living source of InI true identity (being) Christ in his kingly character Haile Selassie 1st came and conquered death and hell, through InI reincarnation and Christ in his kingly character being the resurrection, the I-Soul is invisible to the material eye the senses of object cannot see that soul.

They, the worldly, cannot know or see Ivinity its spirit is materially fuelled and has an existence due to material objects, the spirit that is not of the world is Ivine it is essences cosmic principle fuelled. The world is full of actions repeated to maintain the same form programme and teaches through the six sense organs and the objects with the six sense consciousness attachment to the body feelings, perceptions mental formation and consciousness are all called self (you) the formulation of those dissolving things are considered to be self (you) in the worldly teachings.

All these change, fade and dissolve and are not Iternal but the I the inner I – I soul Irits of essences cosmic principles are the Iternal I. The ever living I, the I that does not deal in 'death, as InI speak unto the world in these days for recognition of InI Ivine faith, that is a love, "Nyahbinghi the Rapture" of Christ in his kingly character Haile Selassie 1st, recognition of InI faith that InI should be identifiable to those of the world in recognition.

On a whole for unity of all nominations of Rastafari way of life, unity will only be attained through "knowledge of the faith," love and holaness, "faith first" InI that are giving Isis unto the one of the throne of Solomon and Sheba in Ethiopia, Christ in his kingly character, Haile Selassie the 1st.

The Ethiopian Orthodox Church is Christ in his kingly character Haile Selassie 1st church in the world. The Nyahbinghi Tabernacle is the Ingels in *the rapture* Administration.

Nyahbinghi, Ethiopian orthodox, Bobo Ashanty and the organisation 12 tribes of Israel, form a unification, having mouth to mouth conversations, cooperating together, Ivine and world intellect of Rastafari, in order for the honour and worship to Janhoy Haile Selassie the 1st.

In the way the 82 different African countries delegates worked hand in hand coalition, all carrying the faith's name but different tribes. For now the real separation is because of the knowledge, when Haile Selassie the 1st speaks of education 'InI must look first to Almighty God.'

So then the knowledge of a ones faith is first and foremost, many Rastafarians of today that uphold the nationalism, of the Anglophone Caribbean, 'the land in which the body is obtained is their object of worship' that was branded in many ones minds by the gentile colonial master, such nations they worship the dragon and follow the beast, those only love themselves and the gentiles, as they together carry the spirit of the world knowledge.

Under the spell of such designations, they separate and divide, among such it will be difficult to attain Inity because they see variety and not Inity. Christ in his kingly character returns keeping his promise, in a new name Rev 3v12, *'And I will also write on him my new name.'*

Ras Tafari, when a one carry's their locks, Nazarene covenant upon one's head, men and people will call that one Rastafari, therefore the locks is written Rastafari on ones head, that is Haile Selassie 1st name and signature.

Those churches of the world will not for now proclaim the returned messiah until they crown a king in the land they call modern day democracy Israel, until that time the Pope of Rome stands in the place of I Negus I Christ to the world, as the head of the chapel regardless of their denominations.

InI in Ivinity, it is InI soul that must be first for preserverance and identification. InI must see and know InI faith Irits, and hear InI soul before InI know of the world. InI must have InI knowledge of Nyahbinghi, because Rastafari is knowledge, it is vital to know Nyahbinghi faith, for without the knowledge of the faith a one has no faith.

The amount of knowledge a one has of Nyahbinghi, that is the portion, the strength of faith that one has. InI are the builders of InI own destiny, and the results are not limited to the ways of the world, or the concepts of the world. It does not pay to live in illusion thinking that peace and paradise can be found in the world. There is no peace in the world because it is the anti-Christ, the beast and the whore of Babylon queendom; the worldlians are serving, they that run the world for Lucifer, according to their world orders, arms and ammunition. So where is the use that they are running away from King Ras Tafari, Christ in his kingly character?

Many that don't have the knowledge of InI cosmic tradition, their expectations from the "I AM that I AM" is always something purely materially visible, even negative actions that can be seen, that is why many have no hola faith, many faith is a musical in entertainers, those that do not have a hola reincarnation of fire baptism and hola Irits seal, on entering into their faith in Christ in his kingly character Haile Selassie the 1st, those are of the world. For those all that is worth treasuring must be visible and appreciated in Babylon world, those don't have hola Zion's Irits. Zion is King David, King Solomon City, bestowed unto Haile Selassie the1st, the heavenly Zion, Irusalem spiritual sense, also the earthly material kingdom.

Haile Selassie the 1st and InI *the rapture* in Zion, Hebrews 12:v22-24, *'But you have come to Mount Zion, to the heavenly Jerusalem, the city of the living God, the great I AM that I AM. You have come to thousands upon thousands of angels in joyful assembly to the church of the First born, whose names are written in heaven, you have come to the great God, the I AM that I AM, the judge of all men. There in Mount Zion, you cannot give praises to the devil nor worship Satan, there good is above evil, no evil can enter there.'* In comparison to the high point "Pinnacle"

St Matthew 4:v5-9.' a place of temptation, where a one can only acquire the kingdoms of the world, only I Negus I Christ could of resisted those temptations. The worldlians unto the world cast many a spells of illusions in serving their personal sense for gains and rewards.

Those like Balaam, son of Beor, the Mesopotamian, (Num 22 to Num 24). Went after gains and rewards, built a reggae star house in Babylon Rome aided by Prof Nettleford, serving the empires, queendom, putting a stumbling block in front of InI hola Ivotion, distorting the hola drive of the nation of Shem Melchezedek, the children of king Ras Tafari way of life, Ethiopia hola ark of the covenant faith, into the American anti-Christ life for gains and rewards.

Those serving the empires through the reggae house that they have stopped at in Babylon modern day democracy Israel (Rome), domesticated they have become in serving the empires 'grazing on the allowance of the colonial slave masters world, America hired Marley and Median hired Balaam, they both met the same fate.

The Gong they chose to sound was sounding what is in their heart, InI Nyahbinghi in *the rapture* carry the last trumpet. The Shack, Shack that sounds whatever is in one's heart.

Read about the Gong in I Corinthians 13:v 2-3, *'Though I speak with the tongues of men and of angels, but have no love, I am only a resounding gong or a clanging cymbal, and though I have the gift of prophecy and can fathom all mysteries and all knowledge, and if I have a faith that can move Mountains, but have not love I am nothing, and though I bestow all my goods to feed the poor, and surrender my body to the flames, but have not love, it profiteth me nothing.'*

Ones cannot be Nyahbinghì and serve the world or you will be a slave to one and hate the other. Christ in his kingly character Haile Selassie the 1st, and to those that has arrived in authority, InI the Ingels, that came forth with Christ in his kingly character, in *the rapture.*

InI authority is not verified by men and people of the world. InI authority is cosmic powers, authority from the cosmic radiance rainbow encircled throne in heaven and authority in earth, from a place called Zion in Ethiopia camp David ancient dominion Empire, through king Ras Tafari sovereign of the Ethiopian empire, saviour of the world, upon the Solomanic throne authority (Salem), authority in faith in accordance with earth rightful ruler Christ in his kingly character.

Knowledge of one's faith lets a one know their authority, authority from the original ways of the world. Nyahbinghì administration is authority, which can only be given from the tabernacle, at the time of fire baptism and decorations. That needs not proof to the world of material sense, because InI authority grounding is in Ivinity, other authority in Rastafari way of life, that is not of Ivinity is a thing that is on the allowance of the world. Because Babylon world has its system of colonial worldlians authority, that is forced upon the nations in the earth. Haile Selassie the 1st has already represented InI in the world, with worldly honours of Solomon and Sheba.

The Emperor's coronation, King of Kings and Lord of Lords, the conquering Lion of Judah, Ilect of God and with heavenly authority "Christ in his kingly character, the supreme architect in his second advent through cosmic powers. *The rapture* knowledge must be known to identify Nyahbinghì faith, InI, the Ingels that have come forward with Christ in his kingly character, not those that have been waiting for him to come.

InI Nyahbinghì *the rapture* are vegetarians carrying an Ital Cosmic Irits "InI do not eat fish," Ivine livity cannot give thanks to no blood sacrifice. The Hola Mountain cannot be established during the killing of animals and sipping of mannish water. InI don't suck salt this cuts the Ital Irits heights, the Ital Irits is to have cosmic intersection Iritical dominion over evil influence.

Nyahbinghì administration is a tabernacle theocractical administration. Many a ones must sightup and overstand the meaning of a 'separation from the world,' the separation from the world is 'the faith Nyahbinghì', that has left the world behind waiting for the Christ king.

InI have trodden forward in front in front of the world, administrating the faith of *the rapture* of Christ in his kingly character, Haile Selassie the 1st. The prophecy in Revelations tells of Imajesty Christ king Ras Tafari in heaven (the root of David). InI Nyahbinghì *the rapture* joins no organization that is of Babylon world that is never to be remembered any more.

When a Binghiman trodding Nyahbinghì (Mount Zion) Irits joins an organization such as any worldly organization, he therefore has left his office 'Nyahbinghì administration' and has joined the world.

Christ in his kingly Haile Selassie 1st has given authority into *the rapture*, that came with authority even before InI were known in earth and InI are driving the administration, to serve first the throne of the Ethiopian king of kings before the ways of the established world, keeping the cosmic, galaxy principles and in its powers burning up spiritual iniquity in high and low cities, by heaping up logs upon the fire and burning coals that is consuming those inter-world-nationals, aimpes, false witnesses that are giving false testimonies.

On account of living through material object sense that gives them the spirit (Irits) of the world dead senses of the world, living without Immortality outside of Ivinity with their intellect glory which is their shame , they run to the negative net of objects and senses of the world but they are dead to Christ in his kingly character, without hola Irits (heavens) these are the living dead ,vampires of the biggest vampire barons of Europe.

Chapter Nine

Shem, Ham and Ja-pheth

Genesis 9 v25-27, *'And he said, Cursed be Canaan; a servant of servants shall he be unto his brethren. And he said, blessed be the Lord God of Shem, and Canaan shall be his servant. God shall enlarge Ja-pheth and he shall dwell in the tents of Shem; and Canaan shall be his servant.'*(Canaan is the son of Ham)

The dwelling of Ja-pheth in the tent of Shem is the Gentile impersonation of the Black Nazarene, I Negus I Christ as a white Gentile.

Marcus Garvey in America was a Baptist minister, founder and president of the Universal Negro Improvement Association (UNIA), at the time of his height, before he was betrayed by his Baptist students, who were lesser ranking officers of the UNIA.

Those as Elijah Mohammed and Dr Dobious just to name the two who conspired with the USA government and betrayed Marcus Garvey, then converted 'railroaded' the UNIA into the beginning of the Nation of Islam in America. Those that stole the Black Star Liner money then used it to build a mosque in America.

Many who were among the back to Africa were now to Mecca, because of their greed for a few personal powers and not knowing themselves being in the belly of the dragon of the beast, whorehouse administration, which they themselves were organs of, on account of illusions produced by the world church, state, and sovereign world Rome, wanting to do something to show their worship, to please the colonial masters, and the 'not original Jews' (from Rome's rampage in Irusalem), in the time of I Negus I Christ, even from before and after.

Many allowed the gentiles to trick them into converting to the Islamic faith. Because the Arabindians who that faith belongs too, had already acknowledged themselves seeds of Ham, and accepted the position in life of being Ishmaelites, as Ishmaels mother Ha-gar was an Egyptian Hamite, Ishmael who wasn't the royal promised son of Abraham. They the Arabindians couldn't let it be known in the world that InI the blacker man, of the linage of Shem in earth, are the seed of Isaac.

Therefore they conspired with the roman colonial masters who are the seeds of Ja-pheth, and promoted the gentiles as if they were the seeds of Isaac, now in that the gentiles had impersonated (stolen) what is of InI faith and made religion.

After transferring the image of I Negus I Christ 'the black Nazarite in to a white gentile boy, with long hair and blue eyes, the gentile has stolen that identity, 'saying that his nation is from Isaac, but in truths its InI the blacker man of Shem.

That's how they have stolen the faith that's in the world as theirs, and the Arabindians have agreed with that upon to this time, 'through the camp David agreements'. Camp David in America is still stealing even today the black man's heritage, saying that they are the Royal Family of Isaac Abraham's royal son and the

Arabindians are his illegitimate sons through Ishmael, the son of Abraham from Hagar the handmaid of his wife Sarah.

Now for the black man in America to accept the conversion of UNIA Baptist to Islam, and to give up and worship with a people that hated them as much as the gentile or worse, because here now was a people that accepted that the Arabindians, who are a servant of servants in value to the gentile because of Isaac and Ishmael, now the Arabindians had a people to admire them and join them, praise with them in their lesser value of Abraham's promise, believing that the Arabindians had preserved something, that they though they belonged too.

That was in fact sending them further back in more confusion, (Babylon) being lost not knowing themselves. Because InI in earth the black man are from the children of Shem and family to Solomon the real Jew, descendants of the Queen of Sheba and her only son Menlik 1st, unto Haile Selassie the 1st of Ethiopia.

Islam is a violation to InI destianic laws. Even unto today as in yesterday, 1916 in Ethiopia, when Liyasu, grandson of Menlik the 2nd married an Islamic woman and built a mosque in Ethiopia, the church councils and the rulers of Ethiopia deposed him from the throne and placed him in prison until the day that he died.

America taking them out of the hand of a shepherd Marcus Garvey who knew the way, 'Africa for Africans.' The American rulers weren't happy because even in Holy Wars in the world, the Muslim Arab or Indian would have to acknowledge Isaac superior to Ishmael. That is where the judgement of the present time 'today' is, 'the judgement of Shem, Ham and Ja-pheth,' the nations of these three.

InI the African the black man on earth is of Shem, the Arabindians and the mix race of yellow are of Ham the white man is of Ja-pheth. Whatever religious group a one joins in earth cannot take that one away from the judgement belonging to the nation that they are from genetically or formed genetically.

As religious denominations of the world are open to any and every one, only the faiths that are not of the world are not open to any and every one. "Zion gates are not open to a worldly spirit, even should a one with worldly spirit (Irits), arrive in a Nyahbinghì Igregration, without fire baptism that one will be in the crowed of worshipers but outside of the Irits of Zion I. I keyman who carries authority opens Zion gates in reincarnation fire baptism, through love wordsound, and the powers of the supreme architect.

To be in Zion gates in that presence, to receive that cosmic radiance principle, many will not receive that Iration, to be able to reveal it and what's therein without Nyahbinghì fire baptism. *I urge ones to go down to the foundation, to the Nyahbinghì tabernacle for fire baptism.*

I recommend the high priest fire Ingel warrior, the elderly Prince Nang Nyahbinghì tabernacle because administering Ingels that have been exalted closer to the supreme architect, Christ in his kingly character, Haile Selassie the 1st. Those Ingels have more love, higher knowledge and skills.

The judgement in earth is of nations according to genetics, as peculiar is strange, not known to the world, InI faith Nyahbinghì *the rapture* is a peculiar faith to the world therefore those of the world will not enter therein. A long time ago the Muslim Arab conquest had conquered some African countries, today African people calling themselves Muslim, true enough for it was a black African man name Bilal that taught the prophet Mohamed, but judgement is according to your nation from Shem, Ham and Ja-pheth.

Many of the black people in the world today the lost and gone astray, true descendant of Shem, Isaac and Israel, would use any vehicle that bears resemblance of being freer from colonial satanic teachings, and opting to Islam will still be doing the work of another man.

These who have jumped onto the wagon of the illegitimate son of Abraham whom Abraham sent away even to die in the desert; they with the help of the American dream are running away from King Ras Tafari, Emperor of Ethiopia the returned Christ in his kingly character, descendant of King Solomon the true Jew.

Marcus Garvey in 1935 at the time of the Italian invasion of Ethiopia was printing newspapers that got around the world, Haile Selassie the 1st, fought on the battlefield with the Ethiopian warriors against the invading Italians, through the neglect of the League of Nations not taking effective actions, in 1935 Ras Tafari sought exile in England for the Ethiopian Royal Family, Marcus Garvey was then printing in his newspapers worldwide, articles conveying messages questioning Janhoy Haile Selassie 1st Ivinity.

Marcus Garvey being the one that prophesied the coming of Christ in his kingly character, was then doing the same or similar thing as John the Baptist who had prophesied the 1st advent of I Negus I Christ, then questioned the works of Ivinity, St Matthew 11:v3, *'And said unto him, art thou he that should come, or do we look for another?.'*

Again, Marcus Garvey stated before his physical dissolvent, "When I am dead and gone look for me in the wind and the storms." Telling InI the truth about his cosmic inheritance unto Eternal Life where he will be with InI in this spiritual war. InI Nyahbinghì *the rapture* is InI only true living faith of Christ in his kingly character, Ras Tafari Makonnen Haile Selassie the 1st Emperor of Ethiopia, the blood and the flesh of King David and King Solomon of Irusalem.

Solomon was king, priest and prophet according to order given to the children of Israel and Judah from the great king priest prophet Shem Melchezedek. King Ras Tafari 1st is InI daily sacrifice, all InI treasures are in Mount Zion (heaven cosmology), of earth, 'a place called Zion in Ethiopia "camp David ancient dominion empire". Those songs, Nyahbinghì songs of worships, these are songs that are not of the ways of the world.

Redemption means rescued, released, 'freeman' from the seven seals of material consciousness (material sense), become stronger and greater than the spirit of the world. InI must stay in the Nyahbinghì administration, walk in the administration stay in the truth, sight up *the rapture* or the Binghì will backslide or remain stagnant, in those lands where the faith is an organization, "outside of reincarnation is termed organization" without reincarnation ones are outside of Mount Zion gates, the Ivine livity is within Zion gates. InI are forever trodding up forward in the administration.

Remember the way of the administration that says "Haile Selassie 1st is waiting for InI beyond the seven seals." For the prodigal sons and daughters, who had been anglophiles must now return home in heart, soul, body and mind in the Ethiopian language Amharic, 'prodigal' means "money pleased me."

The world can annihilate an organization, but a faith of Ivine livity it cannot touch. In this time the way to be separate/sanctified from the world is to renounce the world, avoid excessive worldly living, reject the success of all means of the Babylon world, InI self-reliance through knowledge and grace.

Live today, give thanks and Isis to have the precious breath of life everyday tomorrow, from Christ in His kingly character Ras Tafari, Haile Selassie the 1st. The Nyahbinghi Administration is of camp David ancient dominion Empire, Mount Zion is in *the rapture*, Mount Zion is InI dwelling place, Haile Selassie the 1st reign in Mount Zion.

Live to the Nyahbinghi administration, *the rapture* according to Christ in his kingly character, and carry abreast I Negus I Christ in his first advent, fulfilling the prophecies of the prophets of old, knowing that Haile Selassie 1st has represented InI in the world, where InI could not of reached, because of worldly standards and world powers.

The Rapture Ivine Livity, Nyahbinghi state presence in earth is an Ivine Livity alongside mortal livity, as a state within a state materially, but Iritcally two different livity millions miles away from the other the living in Christ in his kingly character and the living in/of the world, walking on earth.

Theocracy amongst the world of democracy is two different states/livity, Nyahbinghi *the rapture* is not a world movement in politics, ones cannot live Nyahbinghi according to the world, Haile Selassie the 1st did not practice (live) Nyahbinghi in his worldly, stately affairs . Even though he was chosen and recognized as the Black Messiah, head of the Nyahbinghi (in Moscow, Russia 1930).

Democracy, a form of governman, a way of putting appointed leaders before God. Democracy teaches of leaders, Earth Fathers that has the power to allow physical life or death. Democracy has cut off the way of theogony, 'the way of God.' And the democracy man has taken the authority of human value into the hands of their selected team, ranging from race, colour and class, I Negus I Christ taught theocracy.

The theocracy: the Commonwealth of Israel, son of Isaac, son of Abraham, known as the children of Israel and Judah from the time of Moses, Joshua, until Saul became king, then in the Invocation of I Negus I Christ Orthodox Christianity unto the appearance of Christ in his kingly character Haile Selassie the 1st.

Every ones following the Christ in his kingly character is of a theocracy, therefore, from democratic a word from demos (demon/Satan's fall to earth). The people power rule (not God), those that have formed the modern day Sini covenant at Camp David in America, 'they plot against God's anointed ones.'

The chosen ones that were chosen to accompany Christ in his kingly character, within *the rapture* ascend of the 2nd advent. Nyahbinghi children of Ras Tafari nation, the nation of Shem, to destroy InI as a nation, that the name of Israel and Judah (now called Rastafarians) be remembered no more, and the original ways of the world be forgotten (theocracy).

The Romans knew that in their democracy that Christianity would not survive in truths (in the proper way). They took the faith as hypocrites because they saw the power of it, and took it in their greed because of the wealth it would bring, so through democracy they would be god, the same Zeus, the Athalian god of the sports world father of Diana/Artemis who fell from Jupiter and is worshipped by the entire world.

Including the organisation 12 tribes of Israel, having not a hola pilgrimage in earth they are of the world. The 12 tribes of Israel organ are the nomination that represents Ras Tafari in the world also worships in the ways of the world. All the affairs of the world is onto the 12 tribes of Israel also the EWF, those administer central worldly administrations that are about man and woman, ones must not hold it against the 12 tribes of Israel because they have gained and enjoyed all the pleasures of the world, those have gained the world at the cost of their soul, the worship of Haile Selassie 1st is not in the world.

The central administration exists on the grace blessings of the Ivine administration. The spirit (Irits) of the world is also a knowledge among the things that it teaches that if you have white skin it is superior to black, those that carry the spirit of the world that is their portion; their spirit is of the world program, so the inferior object serves the superior object.

The Romans in a gang, (the ruling cabinet of democracy same amount in number as the Roman gods), their parliament under the name of Christianity, whilst they aborted the real way, introducing a mysterious, incognito, gentile, pagan, philistine, heathen teachings calling I Negus I Christ name in their satanic world.

Theocracy and democracy would never be one, true worship has to go through an emperor king, that is chosen, by the I AM that I AM, a hola righteous livity cannot be practiced administered whilst living in a democracy. No priest or prophet can come out of Rome's democracy Psalms 147v19 & 20, *'He has revealed his word to Jacob, His laws and His decrees to Israel. He has done this for no other nation: they do not know his ways. Praise the Lord.'*

The reason to why Rastafarians have no leader other than Christ in his kingly character is because InI is not in a democracy. InI are with the supreme architect appointed of the throne that was given by the I AM that I AM, InI are following the way of Christ in his kingly character, Ras Tafari the one and only leader.

InI are not as stately representatives, because this world is not InI home, redemption also reincarnation is not a part of the world programme, redemption is not a worldly thing, the world term for redeemed is captivity, forIver confusion, in which ones live doing another man's will, and not the will of the Supreme Architect.

Mentally chained in democracy and not redeemed through theocracy righteousness, bringing everything to Christ in his kingly character.

The living Haile Selassie the 1st, through the Nyahbinghi tabernacle administration realm in earth, a place called Zion in Ethiopia Camp David ancient dominion empire. The one mediator and same one and only father, the same Hola One, Supreme Architect, Haile Selassie the 1st, is the only leader in theocracy also in cosmic laws, king Ras Tafari earth rightful ruler.

Theocracy 'a means of administering in which priest, prince and prophet administer, Ivinity in righteousness through cosmology, that Ivine administration developed in the name of The I AM that I AM.'

Realization knowledge is through education (knowledge) of self-realization of true self, the 'I' and tradition. Iditation Irits is a dualism of what is the I self and what is not of the I, the self-spirit is inactive 'visually' and bondage of the material concepts, and redemption do not belong to it in the reality of the material world. Love for ones Iternal soul is self-realization.

When one is forgetful of his or her real nature, s/he obtains education/knowledge. InI true self is within *the rapture*, of Christ in his kingly character known only through the fire baptism, to overstand Nyahbinghi faith ones have to know *the rapture* pilgrimage.

InI journey to hola Mount Zion, 'the Rastafari house' Ethiopia InI sacred place, only in the spirit Irits of Nyahbinghi *the rapture* can InI share InI inner Iiverty 'knowledge' become oneness, because on this physical plain InI could be separated, that is why I say InI, and only through love of the fire baptism will InI truly be one heart, one love, one trod, one journey, one administration, Nyahbinghi administration *the rapture*. The Irits of Nyahbinghi lives forever.

Those who claim to be Nyahbinghi but are followers and don't have the Irits, those are they that are shut outside of Zion gate; those will faint, when they face the fire (justification) of the cosmic principles. Nyahbinghi faith can only be known fully through *the rapture*, which is creation and the present future. To know the spirit one has to have the light in their eyes of the spirit, seeing the light that is unseen to others.

Chapter Ten

Christ In His Kingly Character

THE RASTAMAN CREED

Prince and Princess must come out the Egypt, Ethiopia shall now stretch forth her hands unto Haile Selassie I, O thou I am of Ethiopia, Ras-Tafari I and I spirit come unto the I to dwell in the path of truth, lead us, teach us love and loyalty on earth as it is in zion. Help us to forgive that we may also be forgiven. Endure us with wisdom, knowledge and overstanding to do the I will, the I blessing upon the nation: Let the hungry be fed, the sick nourished, the naked clothed, the infant protected and the aged cared for.

Deliver us from the hand of the enemy, so that we must prove fruitful for these first days, when all our enemies are passed away and decayed, in the sea, or the belly of a beast, I and I pray the I to give each of I and I a place in the I King both now and forever so I and I hail to the great and dreadful I, Haile Selassie I. Ras Tafari the mighty eternal I, Haile Selassie I.

Ras Tafari, the unconquerable, everliving I Haile Selassie I, Ras Tafari, A Man

Nyahbinghì main Iritual Iviction is that Haile Selassie the 1st is Christ in his kingly character, InI saviour redeemer, King Ras Tafari. Revelation 5:v5, *'behold the lion of the tribe of Judah, 'the root of David hath prevailed to open the book and to lose the seven seals thereof.'*

Revelation 19:v16,*'and he hath on his vesture and on his thigh a name written, 'KING OF KINGS AND LORD OF LORDS conquering lion of Judah.'* Overstanding that knowledge truth is the way to redemption. Nyahbinghì way of life is in the Nyahbinghì tabernacle administration service songs and InI Iritical Ivictions are in 'the precepts of the house of Nyahbinghì.'

Nyahbinghì *the rapture* are the Ingels society, administering in a place called Zion in Ethiopia 'camp David' ancient dominion empire that travels with Christ in his kingly character where ever he goes.

InI are a portion of the whole fullness of Haile Selassie 1st, 'the power of the hola trinity' that was not revealed in the world because the world is the material kingdom of man. The way of redemption is the fire baptism that transcends all perceptions that make the world.

The reasons of perceptions are object orientated, whereas hola visions are visitations of essences cosmic orders. There ones are focused 'in Zion, transition' in no worldly ordinary state of Isciousness, hola visitations are invisible to the material sense eye, as the ancient prophets would of said *'I was in the spirit' (Irits).*

Christ in his kingly character Haile Selassie the 1st and InI Nyahbinghì Ingels *the rapture,* has come forward in earth to fulfil the prophecies, clarify the administration and accomplish, the renewal of all things.

Timothy chapter 6:v15-16,*'which in his times he shall shew, who is the blessed and only potentate, the king of kings, and the lords of lords; who only hath immortality, dwellings in the light which no man can approach unto; whom no man hath seen, nor can see: to whom be honour and power everlasting.'*

If one cannot, for whatever reason recognize to accept Haile Selassie the 1st Ivinity through I Negus I Christ, king Ras Tafari, direct descent from King Solomon, the Royal Jew of Jerusalem, gives Haile Selassie the 1st the divine right to rule earth, that right was handed down to Judah of King David, King Solomon, the chosen sovereign throne of the I AM that I AM people, the I AM speaking to David Acts 2v30,*'And knowing that God had sworn with an oath to him, That according to your flesh, and according to your blood I shall rise up Christ to sit on your throne.'*

Therefore, the Supreme Architect chose King David's throne for his own sake and glory, so those that fight against that fight against God. Fear not for the body is born that is destined to be vanquished today or tomorrow. Taking to the trod in all seriousness means cannot concern Iself for the cares of the world, because ones have left the world and now is in front of the world, one's shalt not fear knowledge, renewing Irits for recognition of InI loving faith, which will be known in the world as *the rapture,* InI Nyahbinghì.

The Rapture in truths and righteousness is in this time giving reverence. InI Nyahbinghì trod with an undefeated genealogy; it is written chronologically such truths are founded upon a fundamental background, Semitic African Fundamentalism Congo Supremacy.

InI cause in the earth at this time is to rescue/ redeem those of the throne of David, in keeping the promise of I Negus I Christ, returned Christ in his kingly character, Haile Selassie the 1st to bring ones to the prepared place.

First through reincarnation, then repatriation to bring forth ones to the Ras Tafari house, hola Ethiopia land Africa. And forward restoration unto the world to come Iternal through the power of Christ in his kingly character, Imperial Imajesty Emperor Haile Selassie the 1st.

In truths and rights, for justice in judgement of this world, to see that all democracy and all satanic spirit that is in this world be completely destroyed, trampled down under InI feet.

When a one reaches in Nyahbinghì administration 'camp David ancient dominion empire', from upon Zion hill one will see down into Babylon queendom hell unto all them old polluted blasphemous anti-Christians spirits, duppies, jumbies, leegarus, vampires etc. that possess those in the world, those spirits ones will see them clearly through InI third eye, no more will they be able to mesmerise nor hypnotise through the power of His Imperial Majesty Emperor Haile Selassie the 1st, supremacy sovereign.

He is the first of creation/manifestation from Iration, he is the foundation of creation, he is now the precious ointment, and he is the living and true king, creator Ivine supreme power of InI present days and will be forIver and Iver InI King of Kings and Lord of Lords, Supreme Architect and Irator Iternal. Imajesty Haile Selassie the 1st is InI Rastafari power house, he is the ruler and there is no other than he Ras Tafari.

So InI Nyahbinghì are *the rapture* and representing InI Father Janhoy, InI the fullness of Rastafari ancient Ethiopian way of life. *The Rapture* is the present, future; Nyahbinghì reaches its supremacy at the time of Haile Selassie the 1st's appearance on earth, in his kingly character.

Until that time Nyahbinghì was the unfulfilled promise, at the appearance of Haile Selassie the 1st, brought the appearance of InI *the rapture*, but only identified at that time, being the Ingels who came from the heavens, carrying heavenly irits and spoke for the recognition, and the judgement is from 1930 unto Iternal.

So InI are giving thanks Ituinually for Ivine livity. Through love, through works, through sound, through power, through earthquake, through lightning, through thunderstorm, landslides, tidal waves and all tempestuous, roaring elements from creation to destroy the wicked nations, and set Rastafarians free for redemption and repatriation which is now.

InI can't chat Nyahbinghì to them of the world, it would be something strange to them, and something that they would care nothing for. Visitation, a trance, a vision, in reincarnation, Nyahbinghì tradition will be classified as an altered state of consciousness in the world to those who don't clearly overstand *the rapture*.

Culture plays a great role in having visions, Nyahbinghì is InI only remembrance of InI supremacy of nation and royal Solomanic lineage. InI are forIver a living memorial of InI cosmic tradition, it is a living sacrifice of InI way of life.

Other nations remember their wars and ways of life in films, monuments and celebrations annually. Then Anglophiles take part in giving thanks and honours in remembrance and celebrations where their destruction is been glorified.

They have not accepted the returned Messiah in his kingly character, to them I Negus I Christ has not returned, for them his promise has not been fulfilled, they have not been reincarnated from their worldly bondage, their way has not been prepared, their I Negus I Christ has not returned to receive them, (when will their promise be kept?) They will never accept I Negus I Christ again in the flesh, because they will have to move their teachings into Revelation, and Revelation is against their Christ coming in the sky, in flesh lie.

There they will have to praise the I AM that I AM of Ethiopia, the King of Kings, of the rainbow encircled throne room I AM that I AM, the one Christ in his kingly character that is born in Ethiopia,

Psalms 87:v4, *'I will make mention of Rahab and Babylon to them that know me; behold Philistia and Tyre, with Ethiopia; this man was born there.'* According to the lineage of King David of Irusalem, those false church teachers and preachers will never want to tell ones that the only rainbow throne in the whole world is in Ethiopia.

Those think they can teach that I Negus I Christ's crucifixion was his departure to prepare his great glory; he went to cosmology heaven (paradise) with a dying thief, rising after three days.

He had not prepared that place of promise yet, after three days at that time he made the departure, (Ascension) to prepare that place and return in his full glory.

Crowned 1930 King of Kings, Lord of Lords, conquering Lion of Judah, earth's rightful ruler, Emperor of Ethiopia, the true Orthodox Christian, now Rastafari country.

The Black Messiah, head of *the rapture* Nyahbinghì Christ returned, flesh and blood of King David and Solomon, at that time the place had been prepared and he came to show the way with his Ingels, InI Nyahbinghì in *the rapture*, to gather those that he received from the earth, the Twelve Tribes, the Ethiopian Orthodox Church and the Bobo Shanty.

The Rapture Nyahbinghì are gathering those, for InI *the rapture* came with the Christ king Haile Selassie the 1st in this Iniverse, Nyahbinghì knows the names of those that are written in the Lamb's Book of Life, when he arrived to the Father in heaven from the Ascension.

They were those that were in the earth, to be reincarnated with a heavenly Ingel, essences of cosmic principles forms, Iternal astral body reincarnate into those persons. There at the same time they were in heaven also, but only their cosmic principle Ingel form and they were also the same ones who were on earth, until the day their celestial forms came and reincarnated into their earthly bodies and killed their worldly spirits, that the heavenly principles (life) could live.

So in heaven only the celestial forms were there and when they came to earth, the celestial entered their earthly bodies in the reincarnation, fire baptism, as those bodies were living according to the world, waiting and longing for the strength (gift) from Christ in his kingly character.

Now ones had to know who their celestial beings are, Nyahbinghì is a fire Ingel warrior whose true dwellings is in Mount Zion (heaven cosmology), so InI know the way because InI came together, InI *the rapture.*

When the time of gathering is over, restoration shall take place, do not set your souls on material things because they are not Iternal, material is earthly time, death does not exist, one's true Iternal self, that one's need to know spends only a short time in earthly form, don't be hypnotised and love the world and lose your soul.

Death is a comfort for them it fulfils their overstanding, cease to exist, it is a weak conception that arises from captivity, it stops the Irits from fathoming Iternal principles.

InI are Nyahbinghì, and to the world Nyahbinghì are known as *the rapture.* Christ in his kingly character Haile Selassie 1st has returned, together with InI. King Ras Tafari came forward in *the rapture,* and took the head seat of InI brethren The Ethiopian Orthodox church. InI Nyahbinghì *the rapture,* InI must carry a dreadlocks covenant that is InI daily sacrifice.

Vow to the I AM that I AM, to carry what Babylon world terms as a shame. If ones don't comb ones hair, Babylon says 'you shame them.' InI don't offer a daily blood sacrifice, a Ivine Irits is a Ital Irits, when ones are eating flesh of the blood, they do not carry an Ivine Irits, those are not in Ivinity, not in InI livity.

InI don't eat anything that carries blood, animals, fish, birds, but InI wear a shame amongst the nation as InI sacrifice. Their term of shame is InI glory, InI Isecration upon InI head is Idecated to king Ras Tafari, 'that Idication becomes sacred and hola, the Nyahbinghì Nazarene covenant is the same covenant of the prophet Samuel,'1st Samuel 1:v11, *'I will give him unto the lord all the days of his life, and there shall no razor come upon his head.'* InI ivocation to the Supreme Architect, InI locks is InI communication, the cords of InI hair is onto the I AM that I AM, he is InI strength. So InI is in Iditation commune with the supreme architect, the way fire Ingels should be. InI are Nyahbinghì, *the rapture.*

Many think that Rastafari is about the length of one's locks, that it is not so, Rastafari is a knowledge, it's a strength and is also in how much knowledge a one has of Rastafari way of live.

Those who are not *the rapture* do not know InI cosmic tradition and know not Nyahbinghì true identity of the absolute truths, 'fire Ingel' warrior. Many are in captivity, bondage through the material sense world, and those do not know what redemption is, those they are the living dead, not been redeemed in reincarnation from the world; such are Nyahbinghì in name only.

They are Anglophiles that are caught up in the fascination of imitating, following, impersonating for personal sense-gratification, ego power. Impersonating the once colonial master, still in his slave masterism, he that they had worshipped as master, the one who had them declare him as superior.

The Anglophiles today themselves long for that admiration, and they give their all, through service to Babylon world, as they chase that illusion, given to them by the ways of the world.

The whole world is a fire, demons, anti-Christ, beasts dressed as saints; African children turn Anglophiles, these Anglophiles at the Emmaus Crossroad. They took the road to Mecca, Rome and Canterbury they missed the King's Highway to Ethiopia, what time it is, they don't know, fat time for home, repatriation.

Chapter Eleven

Administration

In InI time *the rapture* times of recognition, recognising InI tabernacle administration, InI gathering, walking in Nyahbinghi Rapture faith, of Christ in his kingly character Haile Selassie 1st, "he whom walketh in the mids of the seven golden candle sticks", there walketh InI also, Nyahbinghi rapture Ingels in the midst of the 'seven golden candle sticks.'

Serving InI accurate identity from amongst the teachings of the anti-Christ dragon, beast, harlot that built their world of confusion in earth, dragnet of false ideology and satanic customs. Truths are if you are not trodding Mount Zion, then you are building Babylon (confusion). Those that carry the Irits of the world their thoughts are always in Babylon, when I Father Haile Selassie the 1st lives in Mount Zion Ethiopia.

Living in captivity a world of evil Rome confusion being attached through cares for any Roman worldly ways, whatever any reasons for cause one is building Babylon Rome.

Things could not be more difficult than they are right now, InI tradition is an emergency because one's material flesh will hold a one to a material sense imperatively, and the world is set on material advantage, on putting down/burning out the material spirit or not living in the sense gratification of the material, one would be redeemed from the subjection of men and people. Through Repatriation InI shall better InI lives.

InI body is born, but the soul is not born our soul has no beginning nor ending. Therefore the soul spirit must be the real forIver living I, the identification of self, when ones say I or me or you. Therefore InI know that the (God) Supreme Architect is mother and father, owner and master of I that lives forIver and Iver. InI saw in earth Emperor Haile Selassie 1st and Empress Menen 1st become one in union.

The six senses the world is built off on, these senses are the gateway to the seven seals, Haile Selassie the 1st lives beyond the seven seals. King Ras Tafari way of life flows from beyond the seven seals, yonder galaxy Ivinity, Imajesty Christ king Ras Tafari has precede on forward, to further this same second advent 'he rises his soul and hides his body' earth's rightful ruler Haile Selassie 1st.

The seals are two ears, two eyes, nostrils and mouth, which are kept by the seven eyes of the Lamb the seven golden candle sticks that burns, equal the seven churches of InI embodied (Temple), that the seven spirit of the Supreme Architect most high 'the I AM that I AM, gives essence cosmic principles service too, (read Revelations).

Before I Negus I Christ "the root of David" was acclaimed in heaven to break the spell of the service of the world that had taken domination of these seven hola gates through hypnotism, sorcery, spells, mesmerism necromancy, wickedness, i.e. iniquity.

Haile Selassie the 1st was is the only one worthy in truths to receive praises, honour and power, the hola one and only one who could break the hold of the world on the seven seals. The world service to the bodily temple that is meant to be hola and sacred Idicated to the creator, is an entertainment, a whore house and an object to be dressed in self-gratification, claiming personality that is not within I Negus I Christ.

InI are the tabernacle (InI are the living nervers) collectively together InI purpose is to glorify the maker of heaven and earth in the personality of Imajesty Haile Selassie the 1st Christ in his kingly character, to live a hola life, putting the will of the Supreme Architect Haile Selassie the 1st before InI own free –will-heart of the Nyahbinghi administration *the rapture* faith before the ways of the world.

The world is Babylon = which is confusion. Haile Selassie the 1st opened the seven seals, *'The way out of the bondage of the six senses.'*

The people were and are bound by the six senses and cannot know that the seven churches of their body temple had seven seals closing them off from the reaches of Ivine truths that are the knowledge of the Supreme Architect and visitation of essence cosmic principles.

They had accepted information closing them into the world and the way and will of men. They acknowledge themselves as a material form, thinking that material is man (all) foremost.

Prince Mammon was vain and could only be prince by material love (love of material) love of the six senses vain, worldly, the mammonist philosophy of "work very hard and enjoy sense gratification. Mammon exalted what can be seen, that confusion became Babylon.

The rivers of Babylon, down by the rivers of Babylon (six senses) the ways of the world 'where we sat down,' held down by the ways of the world, 'leaders and their leadership for their self-gratification.'

After physical dissolution there is nothing for the fleshical body, but there is something for the essences cosmic principles that was blown through the nostrils' of Adam then Eve earthly bodies that allowed them to live after their bodies were formed.

True self-realization is spiritual re-alization, InI Nyahbinghi are the living Isciousness of Christ Ras Tafari, although InI are engaged in certain material activities InI knowledge knows that the body is not the I when I refer to myself nothing of my being belongs to I, but to Imajesty Haile Selassie the 1st.

Whereas the worldly persons are devoted to the body as themselves and live purely for the results of his activities, because they have a false identification of their true self, those are they who do not know their true identity.

Rastafari is a way of life that one's live, to practise Nyahbinghi carry king Ras Tafari everyday always knowing that Haile Selassie the 1st is always with InI the living

Christ in his kingly character Haile Selassie the 1st that InI know it is a Iviction that InI accept by faith.

Faith is greater than material bodily conditions, wealth and riches, for so many people are always asking where is Haile Selassie the 1st? Those are not supposed to know no beginning of days and no ending of time the ever living Haile Selassie the 1st, the man is above material conception, anything that has birth of material also has dissolvent as the body, but the body does not indicate the living I, but a worldly object, the soul spirit is not born, but because the soul takes on a material body the body is of a birth. The soul spirit essence cosmic principles lives forIver, always remaining the same, whatever changes the body and mind go through.

The rapture Nyahbinghì reincarnation, InI, are carried away from the ways of the world, transcending the mental chains of conceptions, redeemed through *the rapture* of Christ in his kingly character redeemed to praise Haile Selassie the 1st and see through Babylon wrong teachings.

Recognition in *the rapture* each and every nation will praise Christ in his kingly character through *the rapture* teachings, every nation will know the faith because Ingels and men who worship Haile Selassie the 1st have different office, that way his Ingels and saints shall be declared all nations must praise Haile Selassie the 1st, because there are the anointed and there are the multitudes. The appearance of Christ in his kingly character is to separate all nations from each other, for the full effect of pure true spirituality, Imajesty Haile Selassie the 1st words on spirituality (April 5th 1948) 'Spirituality is simply a way of life, pure and original, it embodies our culture, true identity, nationhood and destiny.'

The above are the essence collectively that must call upon the supreme architect in agreement for what they were created for, all ingels and humans are created to serve the almighty supreme architect (known to InI as Haile Selassie the 1st) those who are led by object material sense conception of life, they do not live by the guidance of the almighty supreme architect but through the allowance of men, what men conceptualize to form the worlds thoughts, as those say you don't have to be dread locks to be Rasta (well who will call you Rasta without you having dread locks?) InI are Nyahbinghì are *the rapture* – yes Rastafarians – Haile Selassie the 1st alone is Ras Tafari.

You see many ones speak not of an administration, whether that administration be of the world in Rastafari way of life or not of the world those are self-appointed spokes persons who acknowledge not their nomination, therefore they walk in no administration of Rastafari way of life and are walking in the administration of the ways of the world.

Their administration the whorehouse administration already a worldly thing, they know not of the authority of Nyahbinghì faith, 'Nyahbinghì administration, *the rapture* is an authority of Christ in his kingly character, same one I Negus I Christ as before and forIver. InI way of life is Rastafari, InI *the rapture* Nyahbinghì is the fullness of Rastafari way of life, for those of InI that came with Haile Selassie the 1st in *the rapture* could not mistake HIM for no other.

Conclusion

Complete repatriation will only happen when redemption is attained from the world and that will be at the time of the 3rd wo, world war 3 when Ethiopians (Africans) want to preserve their lives from the neutron bomb.

Zechariah 14:v12, ' *and this shall be the plague wherewith the Lord will smite all the people that have fought against Irusalem their flesh shall consume away while they stand upon feet and their eye shall consume away in their holes and their tongue shall consume away in their mouth.* '

The effects of the neutron bomb.

Glossary

Ivine	Divine
Intents	Contents
Irits	Heavens/Consciousness/Mind/Spirit
Itained	Contained
Idecated	Dedicated
Idication	Dedication
Icentration	Concentration
Ideation	Meditation
Iritual	Spiritual
Isis	Prayers
Ivinity	Divinity
Iternal	Eternal
Ones	Your/Our/Their
InI	Us/Yours/Mine
ForIver	Forever
Iditating	Meditating
Icracy	Theocracy
Overstanding	Understanding
Iration	Creation
Irusalem	Jerusalem

Batawi	Priest
Nimpes	Devils Disciples
al	Bloodless
ini	Mount Sini
ect	Elect
ation	Creation

From Africa to the West, this book belongs to the House of Nyahbinghì